My Lι
is a
Time Capsule

by

Dr Richard Wood

2016 ā veɳ best wishes

Richard

UNDEAD TREE

ISBN 978-1-898728-30-6

1 2 3 4 5 6 7 8 9

Dedicated to my wife,
my three children
and four grandchildren.

Contents

Acknowledgements 7

Foreword..9

The Time Capsule 11
    Henry VIII's affair revealed as lute is repaired............12
    Why build lutes but not play them?.....................13
    Flight MH370: relatives to offer £3 million 16
    Paxman's put-downer 18
    The Brunswick Inch: units in the Renaissance............18
    A pointless California hotel 19
    The Duke of Ellington 22
    What is Jazz? 22
    Poisoning of Alexander Litvinenko 32
    Heroin addict Alice and a Masai warrior 34
    World's biggest egg – really?.........................37
    Missing teen found alive after "abduction" 39
    Deliberate self-arrest in North Korea 40
    Suggested casting for Lenin story.....................43
    The Breakfast Chef 43
    Trump...53
    "Demon Barber" slashed neck but spared jail 54
    Police bike stolen, thief falls off 56
    Price of Christmas dinner slashed by stores 57
    No shred of wit in Jericho.............................58
    "Gangster's moll" jailed 59
    TV soaps promote NHS time wasting 61
    God on the phone.......................................62
    Daughter charged with stealing from mother 63
    Men who are victims of women's violence 64
    Does a girl have to be pretty for science?.................67
    Janner, Establishment and cattle prod............70
    War Book commended.....................................71
    Lawyers: how they build their reputation...................72
    "Putin is destroying Russia" 74
    Atheism in education 80
    Atheism in schools.....................................84
    End secrecy of confessional – Archbishop 85

Booze-fuelled strip on London Underground 86
Stalin's atheism..87
Political boundaries torpedo local identity 88
Simon Raven (Part One)..91
Simon Raven (Part Two)..93
To the Alliance of Green Socialism local rep 97
NHS doctor flees UK to join Taliban...........................98
Penguins liaising with seals...100
Inquiry into historic child sex abuse...........................101
How to remain cheerful with all around 103
Beliefs: atheism must be reflected too.......................104
Play: "Piano man" washed up on Kent coast.............105
The Exclamation Mark: a personal viewpoint...........109
Can a poker hand be life-saving? 111
Ignored WhatsApp text message – divorced 117
Climate change report: "...could do better" 118
Two hundred and forty-nine miles...............................119
Saudi husband sees wife's face for first time.............120
Tory MP murdered a boy at an orgy – claim 121
Child abuse enquiry: continued disarray 122
How safe is mouldy food to eat? 124
The Sex Change Spitfire Ace..125
Spacecraft to rendezvous with comet 126
The lute's social status...129
London brutal beheading 130
Probe lands on comet..131
Bodysnatcher turned murdered daughter into a doll...132
Birth of an aircraft 136
London Spy..138
Mansion tax criticised..139
The real private life of the lute 141
Dwarf stripper gets hen night bride pregnant 142
Libya crisis: rival militias position themselves 144
Humour...146
Can you really be born evil?..151
The Chancellor likes to keep his fridge locked 154
Lute and sarod...155
Not good for dinner 158
"Strict" Catholic school – tattoos banned.................159
Royal pardon for Alan Turing.....................................160
Catholic Church and Nazis in Argentina 160

5

The properties of Lignum vitae 162
Prof Stephen Hawking: England's chances 164
A computer hacker walks free 166
Visulate: birth of a word 168
Mapp and Lucia 171
Rising Damp..171
How to stop motorist driving the wrong way 172
Pope rents out Sistine Chapel to Porsche 174
Hurricane Gonzalo and Network Rail 175
Hurricane Gonzalo: 75 mph winds to hit UK 176
18,000+ requests to remove Google links 177
A mind-reading device..178
Professional wit – deludes many people....................179
Experts blast "medical tourism" 181
Life in Squares..183
Why daughters cost £5,700 more than sons 184
Returning a forgotten book 185
Zombie – self inflicted RTA..186
Leonardo self-portrait 187
Inflammatory beheading story....................................188
Fag-end..188
Carbon fibre and musical instruments 191
Community radio appearance 194
Mars mission one-way..196

Acknowledgements

Heartfelt thanks are due...

To *The Times, Daily Express, Daily Mirror, The Sun, Daily Mail, Mail Online, The Guardian, Sunday Guardian, London Evening Standard, The Telegraph, Sunday Telegraph, The Spectator, BBC News, Northern Echo* and (much lamented) *The Independent* for curious snippets of news (now literally "history").

To various other publications, at home and abroad, whose fair-use extracts are acknowledged in their contributions.

To various email correspondents, too numerous to list here, but acknowledged in the entries concerned

To Ian Clark, of *Undead Tree Publications*, for editing this collection of curios.

All profits from this book will be donated to *Freedom From Torture* (formerly: *Medical Foundation for the Care of Victims of Torture*), 111 Isledon Road, London, N7 7JW.
Registered charity: England 1000340, Scotland SC039632.

Foreword

Imagine yourself as a musical and historical academic restorer, working perhaps in the basement workshop of the Victoria & Albert Museum in London's Chelsea. You might be dissecting a sixteenth century lute donated by a German philanthropist, in whose family it had laid untouched for a very long time. During the sixteenth century many German instrument builders migrated over the Alps to glean knowledge and experience from that cutting-edge of such technology in northern Italy – Cremona.

From their earliest days lute builders have used all sorts of miscellaneous scraps to strengthen their fragile internal rib joints, the ribs being only 2-3 mm thick. Such scraps might be anything from an unpaid bill, a soaked-off bottle label to a tear-off from the wife's underwear – none have the slightest *musical* relevance to the instrument itself. *I've* actually used linen because it's very strong, yet couldn't resist the temptation to add a variety of "inclusions" for a very good reason. Stringed musical instruments have always, and always will be, built using hide glue because it's reversible with boiling water and a hot knife.

Such instruments have a long life (barring destruction) defaulting to hundreds of years. And during that life they will almost certainly at some stage need repair, modification or occasionally pure historic inquisition. For example, the V&A employ staff whose job is just that, and their results are often published in the appropriate public domain, in the same spirit as scientific papers.

It might surprise some to know that *The Lute Society (UK)* has members in New Guinea and Paraguay while *The Guild of American Luthiers* has always had world-wide membership. The ambient climate of South America will invite repair often enough.

For any repair or investigation for whatever reason the first thing is removal of the soundboard, and what is revealed? First the luthier's name, signature and date. In this case ♥ is my signature. Then in addition is the structural augmentation mentioned above. Because I've used linen strips my "inclusions" are cosmetic rather than structural, but nevertheless I feel that they are important for their own quite additional reason; remember when you last moved house, what was under the old carpets?

Here, in the year 2216 for example, our imaginary but perfectly realistic V&A restoration technicians might well discover whose colleague's wife a prominent politician was having a sexual liaison with five hundred years earlier. This is not as facetious as it might sound as newspapers live on such scoops, and collectively these snippets reveal a "time capsule" reflecting life contemporary with that of the luthier. And this is little less than a gold nugget for the investigative musical historian, not to mention the *current* contemporary press along with its readers; an extreme case might even jolt the history book authors themselves into a little editing.

Richard Wood,
Staithes, 2016.

10

The Time Capsule

Here follows (in no particular order) a host of snippets for the lute under construction, including the best of those that didn't quite make it into the lute itself...

Henry VIII's affair revealed as lute is repaired

Finish of a lecture during the Staithes Festival of Arts & Heritage, 2013.

A vivid time capsule contemporary with that of its builder: the early twenty-first century.

Let me take you back five hundred years. King Henry VIII has six wives. Amongst their inevitable children it's a near statistical certainty that almost some will be girls. Henry, being who he is, it's also almost a near statistical certainty that he's got one of those daughters up the dosh. She's, say fifteen years old.

Now he's obviously not going to let this get to the ears of any of his nearest courtiers. And the Press – heaven forbid. (Remember there have been newspapers since the fifteenth century and from whom did our current cynical hacks learn. They'd have a field-day here).

Yet he feels he's got to get it off his (even his) chest. Well, often while hanging around waiting for opportunities to partake of his extra-marital recreation, he's forced to put up with tedious recitals from a small group of musical players. So where do they get their instruments? Who makes them? He wonders. Whoever they are won't know anyone amongst his personal entourage. Yes – perhaps a confidante lies here.

Sufficiently distanced from the household there must be makers of those instruments that bore him so much. A luthier, who through no intention of his own, happens to come by way of information of no interest to himself, the imminent royal incestuous baby, yet totally irresistible. And so it finds its way to join the other bits of miscellaneous junk, unpaid bills, newspaper cuttings, a tear-off from the wife's underwear, whose sole purpose is to strengthen the fragile 1/16 inch interior rib joints of his lute's body. To be discovered many, many years later; a bit of totally useless information, yet riveting, not only to our historical musical instrument restorer but to everybody, because it completely bypassed the contemporary mainline press.

And so my invitation (to my audience): "Would you like to contribute to my lute? Brief, humorous, some placement of the date very roughly – beyond that, anything goes. Humour ranks highly because it tends to reflect contemporary flavour. I don't think I need say more."

Three did.

Richard Wood
THE GALLERY, Staithes,
14th August 2013.

Why build lutes but not play them?

First of all I must apologise for going on about this lute that's almost finished. This'll be the last you'll hear of it, perhaps till it *is* finished.

Without doubt the question I'm invariably asked is "so do you play the lute?"

"No."

"Presumably you'll want to when it's finished."

"No."

"Surely after all this time making it you'll be dying to see if it works?"

"No."

"That's unusual isn't it?"

"No."

"Why?"

"Because I'm hardly going to spend two and a half years making something which won't work."

"All right, so how do you *know* it'll work?"

"I've made three instruments before, and *they* work."

"Well if you can't play any of them how d'you *know* that?"

"Because I have plenty of friends who do play. And not only do they play them, they *set them up* properly in the first place, which is very important because I don't have the faintest clue about any of that either."

"Well OK, that's interesting. And does it really take that long?"

"It certainly does, because you've got to make various jigs for the main parts, the body, peg box, peg shaver, and these have to be spot on because the final instrument's only as good as the jigs from which it's built. Collectively the jigs take just about as long to make as the lute itself. Of course should I want to build *another* one, then yes, it would be a far quicker."

And so it went on for a bit, but only for a bit because I found myself secretly asking myself the same question.

Of course over many years I've read all about stringed instrument building, contemporary as well as historical. The great Cremonese luthiers of the seventeenth century for example are fascinating. What tools did they use and where did they get them? It's not as easy to find out about all that stuff as you might think.

I mean *Google's* far less help than you'd expect, and lots of things aren't usually recognised. For example the tuning pegs of that Amati fiddle, worth a lot of money now, might perfectly well have been turned by his second cousin's younger brother, though overseen by their luth-bosses. Amati, Strad's predecessor, tutor and mentor, weren't just single people; they were workshops with family and artisans working with them.

I often think they must have had to forge many of their own tools, or had tool-making friends. Making the linings and the very tight c-bouts of a violin body are no slouching matter. How did they do those very tight bends? I use an electric bending iron which caters for any radius, and of course dry. The temperature's around 200°C, measured with an electronic digital thermometer. People always ask: "d'you steam those ribs?" Hardly. I've just spent five years drying them, so I'm not gonna get 'em all wet again.

Anyway that's taken me up a side street.

The irony's enhanced by the fact that when I'm in my workshop I'll always have Mozart, Vivaldi, Beethoven, Rossini accompanying the lathe, while Mick Jagger creeps in occasionally. But there's absolutely no connection whatsoever between playing and building. The idea that there is, is purely because it's the first spontaneous response that ninety percent of people have. But a moment's thought reveals no logic. I love the fine workmanship. A millimetre to me is a brick to a builder. At the same time I'm well aware that a millimetre is not going to make the slightest acoustic difference. I don't care. I just like working to fine tolerances, that's all.

I don't even enjoy any of the lute music I've heard. Can you really imagine all Henry VIII's wives tapping their feet to it. I don't think so. Still less Henry himself.

And in my dreams?

In my dreams Amati would get on one of those high speed trains from Cremona to London, then the one two five to Middlesbrough, the number five to Staithes, stop some bloke outside the Co-op and ask in Italian "where's this Wood fellow live then?" Lindsay would, in deference to Cremoma, give him a bowl of spaghetti, and I'd show him how I bent my ribs. And what does he do in this dream? Well of course he just picks up one of Milo's (Suzanna's husband's) violins, wipes his hands on the arm of the chair, stands up and plays the tune of Mozart's Clarinet Concerto.

15

Well that's playing. I'll just stick to *building*.

RHW

Flight MH370: relatives to offer £3 million

8/6/14.

Family members of the passengers on board Malaysian Airlines flight MH370 have launched a campaign to raise £3 million, which will be offered as a reward to any "whistleblower" that leads them to the plane.

The passenger jet disappeared three months ago today during a flight from Kuala Lumpur to Beijing, with 239 passengers and crew on board.

A huge international effort has failed to find any trace of the aircraft, despite extensive air and sea surface searches, and the use of unmanned drones to scour the Indian Ocean seabed—where Malaysian authorities believed the plane could have crashed.

But many of the passengers' relatives think there has been a cover up over the real fate of the plane, and have told Sky News they now want to raise a £3 million reward in the hope of convincing someone to reveal the truth.

Sarah Bajc, whose partner Philip Wood was on MH370, told the broadcaster: "I'm certain there's been a cover-up.

"I'm not sure who is doing it or why they're doing it, whether it was an intentional act that's being obscured or whether there was a genuine bad thing that happened and people are trying not to let that come to life.

"But we honestly believe that somewhere there is a person who knows something that will allow us to find the plane and find our loved ones."

The cash will be raised through donations, with some of it going into private investigations into any new theories about the plane's disappearance.

Last month, those in charge of the search admitted that the missing plane was not in the Indian Ocean search area where acoustic "ping" signals were heard, with Australia's transport authority saying that search zone had now been "discounted as the final resting place of MH370."

Then last week it was revealed underwater listening devices picked up a "dull oomph" 10 minutes after the jet lost radio contact on March 8, which could have been the plane crashing into the sea.

If this was the case, search crews have been looking in the wrong area.

With conspiracy theories continuing to circulate, no wreckage from the plane has ever been found.

Paxman's put-downer

letters@independent.co.uk, *Friday, 27ᵗʰ March, 2015.*

Dear Sir or Madam,

Those of us over a certain age will without doubt remember Mandy Rice-Davies's aphorism which crept into our language many years ago and still elicits a wry smile: "well he would, wouldn't he?"

I think Jeremy Paxman would be proud to join her with his implied expression: *"do you really expect us to believe this?"* (the italics are mine.)

INDY 27th March 2015 page 9

Reminds me of that iconic interview when David Frost decimated Richard Nixon over Watergate.

Dr Richard Wood.

The Brunswick Inch: units in the Renaissance

Studying the units of measurement used by European Renaissance luthiers is far from easy. Luthiers were pretty much a law unto themselves – but that could be said of most other trades. On top of this, different countries didn't necessarily agree with one another over the definition of the same nominal units, nor even different towns within the same country.

In the early to mid seventeenth century, hotbeds of Lutherie (lute building in particular) were Padua in northern Italy and several towns in southern Germany. The lute of this period had a strong German flavour, but the Thirty Years War (1618-1648), which devastated middle Europe, prompted many luthiers to migrate over The Alps to join the musical instrument building communities of Northern

Italy. Naturally they took their favourite units of measurement with them.

Flourishing concurrently with luthiers were the great Cremonese violin makers, notably the Amati and Stradivari families. One of the most reliable authorities on musical instrument building at that time was the German composer Michael Praetorius (c.1571–1621), Kapellmeister (director of music) to Henry Julius, Duke of Brunswick-Lüneburg. In the second volume of his expansive 3-volume Syntagma Musicum he published a full-sized engraving of six inches of his proposed unit of length, thereby promulgating the New Brunswick foot.

Extensive analyses by various authorities of Renaissance instruments (only a few of which are still extant), along with contemporary working plans and construction documentation, yields a figure of 23.78 mm for one-twelfth of the New Brunswick foot, i.e. one Brunswick inch. This compares with the familiar Imperial Standard inch of 25.40 mm.

This figure is the collective conclusion of multiple investigations of material derived from diverse sources, so it is only an empirical estimate, not a properly-defined standard. However it provides a useful "yardstick" (in a manner of speaking) when reporting the dimensions of Renaissance musical instruments, often to be seen in general discussions on the topic.

RHW.

A pointless California hotel

Daily Mirror, 24/10/14.

Is this the world's scariest hotel? Horror fans attempt to spend a 'blood-soaked' night in a hostel.

Thousands of people have signed up to a waiting list in an attempt to take on the challenge to last eight hours in the hotel. Could you spend a night in a hotel that left you tied up, covered in snakes and drenched in 'blood'? It is a question that an amazing 24,000 people are eager to answer as they wait to try to spend one night in a hotel that appears to be from the pages of a horror novel. McKamey Manor in San Diego, California, has the dubious honour of being named the world's scariest hotel.

A truly interactive experience, visitors travel between four terrifying locations and often find themselves trapped in cages, tied to chairs and awash with 'blood'. Visits to the manor are limited to two people at a time, but they are filmed so spectators can watch on global webcams as hardy souls take it in turn to attempt to survive up to eight hours in the horror hotel. It is a challenge that so far no-one has ever completed, but that has not stopped thousands of fans putting their name on a waiting list to give it a go.

Due to its cinematic nature, founder Russ McKamey, 55 and his girlfriend Carol Schultz make sure no two visits are the same. Russ describes the house as PG-13, family friendly and "like Indiana Jones on steroids."

Participants must be at least 21 and have no potentially dangerous medical conditions.

"Nothing is like what we do" he said, "it's like living your own horror movie. There are four different locations, which have been streamlined for hardcore fans, determined to make it through. I consider the people who take part in these haunts as my friends because I research and spend time with them before they go on the haunt. Everything is very interactive: the experience and challenges are to prove what you can and can't do."

The theme changes every year and participants have been tied, had their heads forced into a cage of snakes, eaten rotten eggs and even been gagged. The whole project is run free-of-charge by Russ, who came up with the idea more than 14 years ago.

"Running the year-round, the haunt, though it has been described as the 'world's scariest', is more about smoke and mirrors", Russ said.

A fan of such horror movies as *Psycho, Texas Chainsaw Massacre,* and *The House On Haunted Hill,* he said that the experience has been known to make grown men cry – each guest has to sign a waiver before going ahead with the haunt.

It has been reported that Russ and Carol have spent more than £300,000 to make McKamey Manor the scariest experience on Earth.

The Duke of Ellington

Edward Kennedy Ellington
More commonly known as
Duke Ellington

By Richard Wood – a very good friend to both Tony and Paul.

In July 1999 the band *Crazy Rhythm* did a tour of the country playing their music, interspersed with narrative. The band was Paul Hares, Tony Wright and Nigel Thomson, the narrative by myself was read by a fourth independent friend whom I never knew. This is the narrative as originally written. Now with special, very fond, memory of Tony and Paul, both who tragically died within a few years of one another.

What is Jazz?

Duke Ellington,
born: Washington DC April 29th 1899
died: May 24th 1974

So who was The Duke of Ellington? Well of course there was no such person. As we all know, the Americans don't have an aristocratic hierarchy, although no doubt they would very much like to. However they do know style when they see it. And so did a pal of Edward Kennedy Ellington – Edgar McIntree – at their high school in Washington, who thought him to be a 'pretty fancy guy', deserving a title. And so he was dubbed *Duke* by his buddies, and it stuck.

Style? So what is style? A white tuxedo? Charisma? Being a negro? If you want political correctness – dream on; you won't find it here and you certainly wouldn't have

found it in the world we're going to look at. These are
nothing more than the clothing of style. We are looking
here at musical style par excellence. We're looking here at
grown-up style. We're looking here at style not seen for a
long time.

Jazz is a form of music which you here tonight are
clearly not only familiar with, but also thoroughly comfortable with; you wouldn't otherwise be here at all. Jazz was
born at the beginning of the twentieth century, and by the
nineteen thirties Duke Ellington was at the eye of the
storm. And musically – storm it certainly was.

Let's go back, looking at the beginning of this century.
In 1897 William Krell wrote and published a piece entitled
Mississippi Rag, generally credited with the first use of the
word 'rag' in the title. Krell was a white bandmaster. It
dovetailed with a dance of the time – The Cakewalk, so
called because it involved couples, inevitably in the deep
south, strutting around the dance floor, alternating with
high-spirited antics, the prize for which was a large cake
donated by the plantation owner, and which had in fact
probably been cooked in the first place by one of the
dancers. At the end it was cut amongst them and shared
out. The Cakewalk started in Florida, and was said to have
originally derived from the Semilone Indians – well do you
believe that?

In the old days the likes of Mozart and Vivaldi com-
posed music that could be felt by the classical audiences of
the day. And of course, two centuries later it still is.

Mozart wrote music that resonated with the human
mind's natural rhythms and because of its continued popularity has earned its title – classical. And also of course,
let's not forget it, like Shakespeare and Dickens wrote for
money; it was a living. The composers Stockhausen and

Shostakovich wrote music that resonated with nobody's mind, and probably never will.

But Jazz? Jazz lies in a different domain altogether. It's often said of Jazz that you'll never hear the same piece interpreted in the same way twice – improvisation is one of its hallmarks. Improvise with Beethoven and you'd be shot. Yet Duke Ellington is revered as one of the most sophisticated and prolific composers of this century. Jazz is like rowing across a river; you can see where you want to get to, and get there you will, but according to the swirls and eddies of the current, by a slightly different route each time.

Jazz, almost by definition, doesn't resonate with the mind's natural rhythms either, but in quite a different way to Stockhausen, which is precisely one of its attractions. You might describe it as a kind of human syncopation – the emphasis within it showing its head in unexpected places; apparently without trying it keeps you on your acoustic toes. The word *Jazz* is reported to be derived from the *Original Dixieland Jazz Band* during their engagement with *Schiller's Cafe* in Chicago in 1916. They were then billed as *Jonny Stein's Band.* The word *jass* was originally associated with the emerging style of music, a negro word from The South, one having strong sexual connotations – negroes in 1900 were not famous for feminism – rather the reverse. *Jass* meant something along the lines of excitement, titillation. Need I go on?

Irresistible Jass
FURNISHED TO OUR SELECT PATRONS
The Duke's Serenaders
COLORED SYNCOPATERS
E. K. ELLINGTON Mgr.
2728 SHERMAN AVE. NW.
Phone Columbia 7842

European classical music could only have been nurtured in Europe, and of course was. Jazz could only have been nurtured in North America, for irreverent innovation is integral to America's nature. And they're proud of it; if you want to build a house on stilts, you build one. You don't hum-and-ha, waiting for National Parks to give you planning permission. Nobody expects it. Least of all 'National Parks' (no such thing of course) themselves. It's precisely the same with America's musical tradition. The asset of the multicultural musical community. Not unique to America, but certainly dominant. And gives a leg up to the evolution of new kinds of music. So it was with jazz.

The gro-bag for the seeds of jazz was a fusion, most importantly, of African and American folk music. So, make no mistake about it – it could only have happened in America. Not so much because America has a more creative culture, but because that's where the most prominent national and social elements that were to make jazz fused. But there's more.

Louisiana has been ruled by Spain and was once a French colony. Scotland and other settlers from The British Isles and other European countries such as Hungary with their deep-rooted musical folk tradition also merged. It doesn't take much imagination to see that any musical witch would have a field-day with her cauldron.

Let's go back. Most of us are familiar with The Renaissance – the great change from the Middle Ages to modern civilisation, which in Italy reached its height in the fifteenth and sixteenth centuries.

But there was another renaissance, not so recognised, but nevertheless did happen. Harlem is in the northern part of Manhattan Island, and was originally a middle-class suburb of New York City. But by the early twenties things were different – it had become a crowded ghetto almost, of black migrants, mostly from The South. And with them they brought their own rest and recreation. The glittering example of which has to be an establishment most of whose musical performers were black. Whose operators were gangsters. And whose other attraction in addition to the music was an abundance of very pretty, exotic girls, wearing little. *The Cotton Club* opened in 1923. And the Renaissance? The Harlem Renaissance.

* * *

Such were the beginnings of the popularity of jazz in general and Duke Ellington in particular.

Jazz is usually associated with negroes, and down-trodden ones at that, with its roots growing from the blues. Well Duke was none of these things. Unlike his national contemporary Leadbelly, who was convicted not once but twice for murder, and pardoned on both occasions, Duke never suffered the indignity of the chain gang. He was middle class and grew up emulating his father's impeccable manners, behaviour and immaculate dress style. But he was black, as was his band, apart from one Hispanic Caucasian – Juan Tizol from Puerto Rica. His mother doted on him and called him 'blessed', which in many ways he was.

In 1918 he married Edna Thompson, but of course the marriage foundered, for the duke had uncontrollable sexual propensities. I make no apologies for dialect here for I quote the man himself; "I was trying to fuck ever since I was six years old. I wasn't doing very much of it, but I was trying and it felt pretty good, whatever it was. I finally got it when I was round about twelve years old." That's pushing it; even Errol Flynn would have to bow.

They had one son, Mercer, who went on to manage Duke's band after his death. Training informally under his father, he wrote, in his twenties, much well known material including *Things Ain't What They Used To Be*. Duke and

Edna's would-be second child tragically died, and Edna left Duke with a parting gift – a long scar on his left cheek, mutilating his otherwise black baby-face, reminding him of the minefield love can be.

And he was indeed a pretty fancy guy – certainly way beyond a musician. An artist in more ways than one; a painter sign-writer , running a sign-writing business by day, doing the clubs and bars by night. So if someone commissioned him do a sign for a concert he'd say "well ok pal, who does your music?" and pick up that job as well. If anyone came in with a request – "would you do a gig for us next week?" Answer: "and who does your signs?"

His only formal musical education was offered by one Mrs Clinkscales, which was a complete waste of everybody's time. He soon gave up, in favour of the infinitely magnetic ambience of bars and clubs. Here it was that he was instantly captivated by his mentor Doc Perry, and as far as he, Duke was concerned, this proved to be seminal for his own music. Ragtime was the sound, and jazz was the genre. For Duke these were heady times.

In 1922 he was gathering the elements of what was to become his *Great Ellington Orchestra* with such musicians as saxophonist Otto Hardwick, trumpeter Arthur Whetsol, banjoist Elmer Snowden and drummer Sonny Greer. They headed for New York to make their fortune. This was not to be, and before long they were back in Washington. But as luck would have it this was not to be either; the young Fats Waller was after a band to play at *Barron's Club* in Harlem, and who did he invite? Duke of course. This time Duke and his band *The Washingtonians* hit the right spot with the public. Although, as there was with all bands, a turnover of musicians, Duke's orchestra captured a number of loyal players. With whom he was to build a very high degree of musical articulacy which he honed over fifty years.

His career started in the age of prohibition, gangsters and prejudice. But to the rescue came a knight in white shining armour in the form of Irving Mills – a songwriter who knew all the nooks and crannies of the music business. It was Mills who manoeuvred Duke and colleagues to become the resident band at *The Cotton Club* in New York City. This involved Duke renegading on his contract in Philadelphia; not the problem you might think. *The Cotton Club's* owners and management were themselves gangsters. All that was needed was Yankee Schwartz, one of their 'enforcers' to intervene with a sophisticated scheme involving a brown envelope propped up with a Colt .45. Duke opened at *The Cotton Club* on December 9th 1927 with his ten-piece band.

Ellington's music might well be described as conversation between instruments – and most eloquent conversation at that. Mozart had a style, as did all the classical composers, of a main theme supported by string reinforcements. That was expected, and that was what was enjoyed by audiences of the day.

Jazz capsized all that, not especially intentionally, but simply because it derived from a culture so different from the classical European soil. It was fuelled by the rowdy clubs, saloons and bars of downtown America. The decibel level of much jazz has often been attributed to necessity created by the noise of its clientele. The same culture has often been associated with brightly coloured waistcoats, and dense clouds of tobacco smoke drifting over the piano. And of course let's not forget that America, in a political mood of such insanity, bordering on Hitler's decision to invade Russia; to pass the Volstead Act in 1920.

Prohibition lasted until 1933 when it was repealed, by which time the entirely predictable damage had well been done. How stupid can you get? The US government had given the syndicated gangster management of *The Cotton Club* in New York, along with Duke, a passport to heaven.

In 1931 after leaving *The Cotton Club*, he produced his (then) most ambitious piece – a seven minute composition consuming both sides of a 78 rpm disc – quite a breakthrough at the time. During the '30s and '40s the *Famous Orchestra* as it was called, toured by rail in luxury; they certainly made money. *Black, Brown and Beige* followed in 1943 and in the late '50s came what many considered to be one of his finest works – *Such Sweet Thunder*, born of his new obsession with Shakespeare. So what would The Bard have thought of an American negro setting his 'music' three thousand miles away in Stratford-on-Avon, England. A far cry from the cotton fields of Alabama. Well he might have been surprised; they shared one thing – improvisation. Shakespeare called it blank verse. The Americans called it *jazz*. Given their respective mediums it boiled down to pretty much the same thing.

Not only money did he make, but latterly was showered with prizes of all sorts, yet in June 1965 his nomination for the *Pulitzer Prize* "for the vitality and originality of his total productivity" was rejected, resulting in the resignation of two of the committee of three.

To quote the man himself – "Fate's been kind to me. Fate doesn't want me to be too famous too soon." But of course he did win the *Pulitzer Prize*, albeit in 1999. His granddaughter, Mercedes, told the press that her grandfather had been disappointed not to have won it in his lifetime. The committee's final tribute was 'in recognition of his musical genius, which evoked aesthetically the principles of democracy through the medium of jazz, and thus made an indelible contribution to art and culture'.

Gabriel Garcia Marquez described an innovative new form of literature to the world in *One Hundred Years of Solitude*, later emulated by Louis de Berieres in his *South American Trilogy*. It's been called (amongst many things) 'fanciful reality'. Duke Ellington could be loosely equated; he also developed a unique vernacular that amounted to a spontaneous conversation between instruments.

Consider a Sunday lunch – a family of ten perhaps. Dominated by the muted melancholia of the father – trombone, with a few sons chatting amongst themselves with saxes and trumpets, another brother, in the cultural sense, quietly trying to separate himself on his piano – and of course – the wife – constantly grumbling away underneath all this – double base. What a cacophony. But of course it wasn't at all, only a normal family matrix. They did listen to one another, although they pretended not to: that's jazz.

You don't normally associate the jazz genre of music with the word composer. Not so with Duke. He was most definitely a composer, along with Mozart and Verdi. Just a different style – that's all. Mozart's music you can anticipate to some extent, especially if you're familiar with his work, in the same way you can, to an extent, anticipate your wife's reaction to a certain comment. Duke? No. He's like seasickness. He might ambush the most robust when least expecting it. He could come at you from any direction he liked, but you'd never know which.

Nevertheless people will be honouring his music in another two centuries just as they are Mozart today. I have to say that Mozart will always have a couple of hundred years on Duke – that'll never change. What if they had ever met one another? Apart from having both dressed eloquently, it doesn't bear thinking about.

Duke Ellington had style. That's how he got his name in the first place. His music was his Sunday lunch; bickering perhaps, but in a way so sophisticated that nobody really realised until they realised that they had listened to it. It was then and only then, that they stopped to think.

His last towering works were his *Sacred Concerts,* performed in, amongst many cathedrals around the world, Westminster Abbey, on United Nations Day in October 1973. *Every Man Plays His Own Language,* and a misty *Things Ain't What They Used To Be* seamlessly woven underneath the introduction to *The Majesty Of God.* That's style.

On that very day his long standing friend and colleague, Paul Gonsalves, had been taken to hospital after an epileptic fit. At the same time Duke had unwittingly embarked upon a direct route across the river this time, unaffected by the eddies and swirls of the current – he was dying.

There was to be no more improvising now. He knew where he was going, but nobody else did. That's not jazz. At the end of the show he danced in the aisles of one of the greatest cathedrals on the planet. And of course, in his own world, he himself was one of the greatest cathedrals on the planet. An outstanding pillar of music – The Duke of Ellington.

Tragedy hit the world of jazz in general and the Great Duke in particular in on May 24th 1974. He was seventy five years old, and will forever be remembered as one of the – if not *the* – greatest seminal influences on the music form, which some of you scientists out there might recognise as the union between fresh water and the metal sodium.

But let's just celebrate and remember him through the heady days of *The Cotton Club.*

That's jazz. That was the Duke of Ellington.

Richard Wood.

Written for the band: Crazy Rhythm,
originally for a 1999 tour of the UK.
(This text "randomly" interrupted their playing.)

Poisoning of Alexander Litvinenko

University College Hospital, London, August 2014.

Alexander Litvinenko was a former officer of the Russian
Federal Security Service (FSB) and KGB, who fled from
court prosecution in Russia and received political asylum in
the United Kingdom. According to his wife and father, he
was working for MI6 and MI5 after receiving the asylum.

Upon his arrival in London, he continued to support the Russian oligarch in exile, Boris Berezovsky, in his media campaign against the Russian government.

In the UK, Litvinenko became a journalist for a Chechen separatist site, *Chechenpress*. Litvinenko wrote two books, *Blowing up Russia: Terror from within* and *Lubyanka Criminal Group*, where he accused the Russian secret services of staging Russian apartment bombings and other terrorism acts to bring Vladimir Putin to power.

On 1st November 2006, Litvinenko suddenly fell ill and was hospitalised. He died three weeks later, becoming the first confirmed victim of lethal polonium-210-induced acute radiation syndrome. According to doctors, "Litvinenko's murder represents an ominous landmark; the beginning of an era of nuclear terrorism."

Litvinenko's allegations about the misdeeds of the FSB and his public deathbed accusations that Russian president Vladimir Putin was behind this unusual malady resulted in worldwide media coverage.

Subsequent investigations by British authorities into the circumstances of Litvinenko's death led to serious diplomatic difficulties between the British and Russian governments. Unofficially, British authorities asserted that "we are 100 percent sure who administered the poison, where and how", but they did not disclose their evidence in the interest of a future trial. The main suspect in the case, a former officer of the Russian Federal Protective Service (FSO), Andrey Lugovoy, remains in Russia. As a member of the Duma, he now enjoys immunity from prosecution. Before he was elected to the Duma, the British government tried to extradite him without success.

At the same time, Litvinenko's father, now residing in Italy, believes Boris Berezovsky and Alexander Goldfarb were behind the murder. Berezovsky was found dead at his home in England on 23rd March 2013.

Heroin addict Alice and a Masai warrior

saschacowen@hotmail.co.uk, Monday, *15/6/15.*

Dear Sascha,

Following our chat this afternoon I said I'd send you a tale you might find interesting – I said it was late 60s but actually on re-reading it was of course later; I qualified in 1971. Forensic science must take you to both the path lab and forensic pathologists – what then got you into selling jeans to people like me? And do print this and read comfortably along with a drink, coffee, whatever you have – much nicer than from the screen.

*** is a great friend of mine here in Staithes and was recently reading a book by a doctor (Gavin Francis – *Adventures in Human Being)* about some of his experiences in hospital casualty departments, and I just said to her I'd jot down one of my own for interest, which I gave her a few days later. We often exchange bits of gossip over a few cups of tea. Anyway I'll pop in when next in Whitby – usually in town at least every week – see ya, Richard…

*** – I can't help but add a little of my own Casualty (now called A&E) experience which seems to fit in well with Gavin's. This is around 1973/4. St Mary's Hospital, where I qualified and where Prince George and Princess Charlotte were born (and where Alexander Fleming discovered penicillin in 1928) is in west London, Praed Street – about 400 yards from Paddington station. In those days it was a pretty rough part of central London, although only about twenty minutes walk from Marble Arch (the top end of Park Lane, which is on the north edge of Hyde Park).

Praed Street was full of interesting little shops like *The Bazaar* in Skinner Street, Whitby (Frank Doyle's which I've often mentioned to you) as well as a large number of brothels. A night shift on Casualty would rarely see dawn without having one if not several prostitutes through its doors for one reason or another. Almost invariably heroin addicts, along with alcohol, hash and the other drugs of the era.

The girls were reliably in pretty irretrievable states, one way or another. Domestic violence/ alcohol defaulted to endemic within their background. Having said all that, they were always perfectly friendly to us doctors and we got to know many on first-name terms – they were always respectful and more than grateful for our help and the part we played in there lives. I have never been insulted by a whore not many people can say that. Mutual first name terms was not uncommon. One I shall never, ever forget.

Her name was Alice – two of her friends (colleagues) brought her in with one other man – a punter, at about three or four am – just getting light, She had a hypodermic needle stuck in her arm, broken off. To do that you'd have to wiggle the needle back and forth several times before it finally snapped.

We tried for a while after locally anaesthetising the area – the *cubital fossa* (inside elbow) the standard site for any IV injection for whatever reason. Through prolonged use, this area becomes chronically scarred and had sustained permanent surface damage, and use shifted to one of the prominent veins of the ankle – the common 'next string' to find palpable un-scarred veins.

Heavy drugs were industry in that part of London. Heroin was street-rife, cocaine and hashish competitive prices and perfectly easy to get hold of. For the police to make the slightest impression they might as well have tried reducing pubs sales of vodka and whisky alone. Anyway Alice was proving difficult, and despite X-raying it, we finally had to resort to shunting her upstairs to theatre for a general anaesthetic. After digging the on-duty anaesthetist from his bed, what would have been a half hour job ended up taking about four hours, bearing in mind the intrinsic nursing staff who also needed arousal to implement all the appropriate theatre hardware.

A few weeks later the same whore friends, with another punter, brought her back to Casualty earlier – about one o'clock in the morning – quite by chance I was also on-duty. This time she was dead. Her serum heroin level would have contributed significantly to Afghanistan's national economy, upon which it relies.

Alice was fifteen years old.

That was forty years ago. Yet when I see huddles of youths in the streets of Middlesbrough, Whitby even, my eyes film over as I remember Alice. And I think of the *Papaver somniferum* farmers and their families of Afghanistan, whose livelihood depends on their crop of that very poppy that killed Alice.

Then in the Kenyatta National Hospital of Nairobi in 1972-ish, I recall a Masai warrior who trotted into Casualty with the end of a spear stuck through his left foot. He trotted simply because trotting is his tribe's *modus operandi* for moving anywhere. The fact that they might get to wherever they're going slightly faster by trotting is of no relevance whatsoever. To collect water from the well for the morning's tea he would trot also. The Kikuyu, their neighbouring and far more educated tribe, who provide, for example, all the nursing staff (usually Anglophone – from Swahili) of the medical community, simply walk. They, completely unlike the Masai, are wholly peaceful. No sooner had we got the spear end out, with substantial local anaesthetic, he just got up and trotted down the length of the ward and out back into the bush...

PS at The Deli, *note ***'s tale* Night Shift – *a poem about a prostitute.*

See you soon, R.

World's biggest egg – really?

Daily Express, 24/10/14.

Heavy as a sack of potatoes and the same size as a beach ball – the monster snack could well be the world's largest Scotch egg.

Creative chef Jon Fell, 42, put his culinary skills to the test by creating this enormous version of the popular bite-sized snack. The extra large treat packed an incredible 8,000 calories, weighed a whopping one stone, seven pounds and was an amazing 18 inches in diameter. It was also big enough to feed 60 people and used an ostrich egg imported from Mexico; it's around four times an adult's average daily food intake. This enormous snack was made using the giant egg – weighing just over two stone – along with one and a half stone of sausage meat, two litres of milk, 32 hens' eggs, and five loaves of bread for the bread-crumbs.

And now talented Mr Fell has his fingers crossed that the gigantic Scotch egg will earn him a place in the Guinness World Records – beating the previous record made in 2008 at just under one stone. He is awaiting an official decision from the experts after unveiling his culinary creation.

John, the head chef at the Sella Park Hotel in Cumbria, travelled all the way to Edinburgh to find a deep fryer big enough to hold the giant egg and withstand the eight hours needed to cook the culinary treat.

"We came up with the world record for the Scotch egg as the previous record held by a chef in London of 6.2 kilograms, seemed doable. I am a judge at The Egg Awards 2014 which promotes the use of local free-range eggs. I'd had a few glasses of wine one night, and thought we needed to do something to grab people's attention; that was wishful thinking – it proved very difficult indeed."

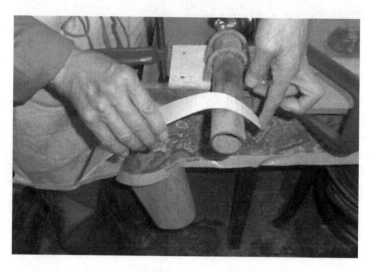

Ironically, Mr Fell's aim of this peculiar project was to promote the use of local eggs rather than buying from supermarkets – but he was forced to import the ostrich egg after failing to find one big enough in Britain. "At this time of year there just weren't any eggs big enough to do the challenge so I had to have one egg sent over. This meant I had only one egg – if anything went wrong it would all be over."

His attempt, in a chip shop in Leith, Edinburgh, was filmed by Scottish Television and watched by an official record monitor and an audience of 60 people. The painstaking task, which took eight hours, started with the ostrich egg being boiled for just over an hour, cooled down with four bags of ice and a litre of water, and then very carefully shelled. Next the chef and his two helpers carefully rolled the delicate egg in the Cumberland sausage meat, while trying not to squash it. Then it took all three of them to transport the egg across two containers, one filled with two litres of milk and 32 hens' eggs, the other with the equivalent of five loaves of bread, in order to bread-crumb the monster. He finished; "There were so many things that could have gone wrong – we could have easily squashed the egg with the 10 kilograms of sausage meat." The trio lowered the huge egg into a fish and chip fryer which was 3ft deep and 4ft wide and cooked it for three hours.

The rules of the Guinness World Records meant Mr Fell could not use a simpler method of cooking the egg in the oven, and had to fry it to ensure it was cooked exactly the same way as a regular Scotch egg.

Mr Fell must now wait an agonising six weeks to find out if his gigantic snack will officially be classed as a world record breaker.

Missing teen found alive after "abduction"

Sky News US Team, 8/9/14.

A teenager who went missing after apparently getting out of her car to help a man who was lying in a ditch has been found alive, and says she was kidnapped.

Police said a woman picked up 18-year-old Hayley Turner standing fully clothed on a street corner in Ecorse, Michigan, 46 miles (74km) north of where she went missing.

She was dropped off at a police station this afternoon and taken to the Henry Ford Hospital in Wyandotte.

Ecorse Police Chief Mike Moore said she was in "good condition" and could not disclose if she had been harmed. No arrests have yet been made.

Ms Turner, of Bedford Township, did not return from a trip to a video store on Thursday night.

Police say she called a friend as she made her way home shortly before it was feared she was abducted.

While on the phone to her friend, Ms Turner said an unknown male had a gun and was following her.

The teenager's friends alerted her father, who sped to the scene only to find his daughter's unoccupied car left running.

Monroe County Sheriff Dale Malone told reporters at a news conference earlier on Friday: "During the conversation, Hayley stated that she was at Dean and Crabb Road when she noticed a guy laying in the ditch.

"Hayley told her friend she was going to get out of her car and check on him.

"Seconds later, Hayley told her friend, 'He has a gun,' and the phone was disconnected."

Her mother, Christy Turner, pleaded with her daughter to come home at the news conference.

Deliberate self-arrest in North Korea

BBC News, Seoul, 18/11/14

In April 2014, American Matthew Miller travelled to North Korea as a tourist. He damaged his visa on the flight and attempted to claim asylum – and he has now told a specialist website covering North Korea that he did his best to get arrested. Why?

There is a ritual to be gone through when North Korea imprisons the citizens of the United States. They are, after all, behind bars in one of the most despotic countries on the planet where the methods of punishment, as described by a UN inquiry include; "extermination, murder, enslavement, torture, imprisonment, rape, forced abortions and other sexual violence."

Every US president would move heaven and earth to get the captive freed. Personal envoys get sent – including in the past, Jimmy Carter and Bill Clinton.

But what if the American captive wants to be there? Matthew Miller who was freed on 8th November is proving to be an intriguing case of the man who chose to defect – though he later changed his mind. He sought imprisonment even when the North Koreans wanted to put him straight on a plane to send him home. "I think it was a mistake but it was successful."

NK News, a respected website which interviewed Miller over several days by email, paints a picture of a "curious tourist" who went on an extreme holiday. He told the website he wanted to find out what North Korea was like beyond the tourist trail. He said he "just wanted to have a face-to-face with North Koreans to answer my personal questions." He didn't explain how getting arrested would help him meet North Koreans. "My main fear was that they would not arrest me when I arrived", he said. As well as damaging his visa, he also produced a set of confused and confusing notes. "I wrote the notebook in China just before going to North Korea", Miller told NK News. The notes said, among other things, that he was a "hacker" intent on "removing the American military from South Korea."

"Perhaps the notebook was a little too much over the top, they instantly knew it was false and wanted to know my true purpose of visiting." In the interview Miller also said he told officials he possessed military secrets, and that the North Koreans knew his brother was an F-35 test pilot for the US Air Force but they didn't seem to care.

When the North Koreans agreed not to deport him, he was held not in some Stalinist gulag but at a big hotel, and then in a guest house – admittedly under lock and key – where a number of other people including fellow American Kenneth Bae were also living. It was only after he was sentenced in September to six years hard labour that he was transferred to a more conventional prison facility, "kind of a farm place", as he put it to NK News.

Shortly after the sentencing, a Reuters report revealed that Miller, aged 25, and originally from Bakersfield, California – had an obsession with Alice in Wonderland, the great work of Lewis Carroll, and had spent two years in South Korea. He had an alter ego – Preston Somerset – a name he used when he commissioned art works illustrating scenes from Carroll's book. 'He recruited a gaming programmer to produce music for him, artists to draw men dressed as Cheshire cats, and a ghostwriter to help piece the whole thing, named *Alice in Red*, together, according to posts on the deviantArt website' Reuters reported.

Miller cited steampunk, a genre of science fiction, as a favourite of his. As well as Lewis Carroll, he also admired George Orwell and Oscar Wilde. So Miller was immersed in a fantastic underworld, but it's more Mad Hatter's Tea Party than James Bond.

Kenneth Bae was released, having been held in North Korea since 2012. Most Americans who get arrested in North Korea are missionaries who weigh up the risks of spreading Christian belief in an aggressively atheistic state and get caught. Robert Park for example, who entered North Korea illicitly in December 2009, and was released two months later, protesting he would rather be martyred.

He says he was tortured, and continues to suffer serious mental trauma to this day.

Suggested casting for Lenin story

letters@independent.co.uk, 4/5/15.

Sir,

Your headline ITN set to expand into drama with stories 'ripped from the headlines' (page 16, 4th May 2015) have been fed with a perfect opportunity, albeit not current, but a producer could make a brilliant two-consecutive-night drama from 2 days earlier (page 9, Sat 2nd May 2015) Revealed: face of the woman Lenin loved most.

Someone as versatile and skilled as Jason Watkins as Lenin, with a woman, Sheridan Smith perhaps, as Apollinariya Yakubova.

That story has to be a T-bone steak for a tiger producer. Readers please – what d'you think?

Dr Richard Wood.

The Breakfast Chef

A short tale by Richard Wood.

Should you find yourself walking past a couple of small hotels in a seaside town anywhere around our coast at six-thirty-ish on the morning of the winter solstice – it would still be dark. As your footsteps crunched the early morning frost you probably wouldn't have given the places more than a cursory glance, and even if you did, nothing much would be likely to register. You'd simply amble on past.

Unless, that is, you were in one of those states unique to us humans; a melancholia commanding you to consider

43

matters normally transparent in day-to-day life, when a more balanced frame of mind shelters you from all things unnecessary.

You might, for example, find yourself lit by the oblique shard of light sharpening the frost in front of you, and stopping to hug yourself from the cold, trace it back to the dimly lit ground floor window of one of them and its sign 'Vac nci s' with its missing letters. And above the door 'B d & Breakf st' again with a couple of voids, and higher still the image of a rampant wild pig with its legend *The Red Boar Hotel* – 'non residents welcome'.

But what of the sound?

The winter solstice on this dawn is completely still and the frost offers you absolute, insulated and palpable silence. Yet not quite.

As you stand in the cold, vaguely wondering about nothing in particular, you find yourself roused from your self-indulgent depths, hearing, sinking through the chill dawn air, the unmistakeable phrases of Mozart's *Clarinet Quintet*. So, despite the cold, despite your melancholia, your mind will not permit you the relief of passing on along the icy street.

For sound, like its compatriot, smell, is a time trans-porter of unimaginable power. And as you survey the al-leyway between the two guest houses with their dustbins over-spilling rubbish of every denomination thinkable, the rotting smell of hotel detritus yields to a vanished world just after the war. The 'Vac nci s' to a vision of that worn maple case battered by years of travelling, and countless exhausted arrivals late at night at just such places as the *Red Boar*. And of course of it's priceless contents, given the hands, capable of evoking nothing short of emotion at its rawest. And even more, of the Cremonese artisans who had built it two hundred years earlier.

You had walked across The Park and Kensington Gardens but in vain was your attempt to relax. How hopeless that had been. And finally standing on the street, looking out over to the tingling crowd outside the majestic semi-circular sweep of one of the most famous concert halls of the world; you had walked straight through them, beneath the shelter of that guardian angel: anonymity. Just one of those many synchronised figures doing their best to implement the work of the great Austrian composer. But you knew, that to be there at all, you had had to be amongst the best. If only those same artisans could have seen their labours still evoking tears two centuries later.

And Mozart? Oh, how you cursed Mozart, shut away on his own, writing, composing at his leisure. You'd envied his privilege. Sitting away in some crumbling ivory tower, inventing an entire world that would be implemented by a cavalry of craftsmen – musicians – yourself included. But then, were you craftsman or artist? You'd wondered, as you'd almost reached the southern border of Hyde Park. He, Mozart ,is the architect; you, simply one of his chisels.

But no. Looking at the geese on the Serpentine, you'd tumbled to the fact that you'd been more than a chisel. You'd been one of his many interpreters. You'd realised, walking across The Park, that artists of any denomination, painters, musicians, writers, all require for their fulfilment a reciprocal intellect from their audience without which they'd be left for dead.

An artist on his own is of little use to anyone. He might just as well stand and talk to himself. So who is the artist? Mozart of course, But, there's always a *but*. You'd pondered; Rubens for example; he demanded only that his audience gaze upon his well-rounded women and enjoy their ample bosoms. But with Mozart it's different. He needs his tools – his musicians – to implement his universe of sound. And there's more: that universe needs to be inter-preted; to be translated so-to-speak. If you happen to be English, Dostoyevsky doesn't make a lot of sense without a sensitive translator.

And so you're safe with her protection – anonymity.

But of course you have no choice. Another tear might freeze on you cheek as you stand in that faint pool of light, listening to the familiar notes, vaguely wondering who the residents of the *Red Boar* had been that night.

Czezlaw usually got in to the *Red Boar* at about six in the morning and after taking off his coat, the first thing he did was pour a cupful of cream, setting it on the floor in one corner. There was a stirring from the top of the old cast-iron range as the huge figure of *Boar* rose, stretched, then leapt with unexpected deftness, landing in a position need-ing no further movement, lapping up the cream in mo-ments, then creeping silently into the morning darkness through an unrepaired crack in the side kitchen door.

He reckoned upon an uninterrupted two hours – sacred hours. Although still warm, he next brought in some logs from under the tarpaulin in the back yard and loaded the range. This usually survived the night, was no problem to resuscitate and the gentle sound of its gradual thermal de-cay betrayed time as closely as the clock above.

There were no residents on that winter solstice. Outside it was cold, but here in his kitchen the range blazed, invest-ing a warmth to his secret world of the early morning that most would much envy. Retrieving a stool and chair from the bar, he set them in line towards the now-open blaze, then reached for the greasy black leather case which lived above the spice shelf. He loved this sacred time on his own.

Now, stumbling past three gas cylinders, you happened upon a ground floor side window of the *Red Boar*. And as

46

the disfigured tones of the second movement of the *Quin-tet* welled louder, you might have peered with caution through the grimy pane. Another tear might have frozen on your cheek as you watched the shadows of the hunched figure, lit by the light of the blazing cast iron Victorian kitchen monument. And the shadow, dancing on the ceiling, turning the right angle and down the far wall, grossly exaggerating the bell of your chef's instrument. Surrounding him: much cooking paraphernalia cluttering a scrubbed oak table, on the corner of which lay a cat whose huge black furry body rose and fell to the oscillations of the opening passage of the second movement. A tap on the window? No, not quite yet. Your flat's only a few hundred yards away.

And now back again past the dustbins, with that very same shabby maple case – a tap? In a moment. Once again peering through the pane, the shadowy figure on a bar stool, music propped up on a chair in front of him. It's now seven o'clock and you're desperate – excited to a point you'd forgotten since you'd walked across Kensington Gardens all those years before.

So – you might have tried the front door, which would probably have been locked at that time. Back between the dustbins? Yes, now, a gentle knock on the kitchen window.

Your figure stops dead in his tracks and the clarinet dies. Through the pane; a muffled "who's that?", in a thick middle European accent.

"Can I come in?"

"You want breakfast? Why don't you come round the front?"

"No no. I don't want breakfast, just to come in. Please."

"All right – use the side door, it's not locked. There's no one here but me."

He's short, stocky, grimy dark trousers, a black waistcoat over a red shirt, sleeves rolled up to almost his shoulder. Round flat face, heavily moustachioed and nicotined, a damp cigarette stuck on his lower lip. A twister of blue smoke rising to the yellow ceiling.

"What on earth do you want then?"

"Nothing, I just heard the music. That's why I wanted to come in. If there's no one staying, what are you doing here?"

"It's warm and quiet. No-one to interrupt ,so I can practice." In his thick Eastern European accent. "Look I don't know you, but if you want breakfast, please just say. Anything you like. Nice change for me to have the company I can tell you."

He'd moved the chair and stool away from the range, music score sliding to the floor, one corner soaking up a pool of oil, and busied himself scrambling eggs, fresh coriander, paprika and frying potatoes with garlic, basil and chilli. Lifting a simmering black iron jug from the range he'd poured two cups of thick black coffee, enhanced both heavily with cognac from the spice shelf, and thrusting one towards you – "keeps the cold out. It's wild. It's winter." And with that, "cigarette…?"

Taking one – "thanks."

"I'm Czeslaw; don't know you of course, but it's very nice to have some company for a change. I came here during the war, and it's rarely I get to talk to anybody these days. Very quiet this time of year, and anyway I'm just stuck here in the kitchen. Mind you, I'm not bothered. I talked to enough people during the war to last me a lifetime. So I just cook breakfasts. Very quiet. For me, the hot soak after the marathon."

You'd asked what he did.

He'd hesitated; "well, I'm a mathematician." And after some time, "and chess – a little chess for relaxation. But I've no friends here who play, so I just think it, but it's hardly the same of course.

"What do (or did) I do? I shouldn't say really, but it can't much matter now. What we did was to dismantle an encryption system. The girls doing our breakfasts to take away in the mornings, always scratted about the dustbins for newspapers to wrap them up, and always found the crosswords filled in, joked about it. Usually *The Times* – they'd whinge – 'it might be a good newspaper,' they'd laugh, 'but it's fucking useless for wrapping your breakfast in.'

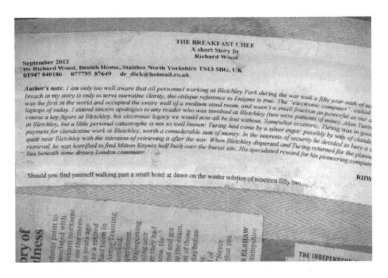

"Anyway this system – clever, yes. Imagine taking an octopus to bits. Lop off a couple of its arms but it'll always grow new ones. The octopus was called *Enigma*. Clever certainly, but with a ticklish armpit. It could never encrypt a letter the same as itself, so for example a Y could be an A, G, an S, anything, but never another Y. A narrow trap-door, yes, but one through which we thin Poles slipped."

"So where are you from then?"

"Well Krakòw originally, but I came over from Warsaw in 1939 with friends. We worked with many of your people, and the Americans, but we got very tired. And eventually, I stayed in England. A few jobs here, a few jobs there, and now I find myself here."

You'd ventured cautiously – "Is there... a Mrs Czeslaw, so-to-speak?"

"In my dreams," he'd sighed.

"So, where was it you worked then?"

"No. We swore an oath; I, we, are supposed to keep our silence but I don't imagine here it could possibly do any harm. A great mansion outside London. We had a huge great electronic computer – took up a whole room. Lots of girls plugging in cables and things all the time. We worked day and night, and not really having a clue what we were doing, at least not in the overall sense."

You'd both sat opposite one another other eating, as the winter solstice wearily surrendered to light. Then suddenly;

"So what's in that case?" he'd asked.

"Well. What do you think?"

"A violin?"

"Yes, you've got it."

"Would you like to play then?"

"Well... Thank you – you wouldn't mind?"

"No no – goodness of course not – on the contrary, I'd be so pleased. So, I mean what do you like? What sort of thing?"

"Mozart? Like you were just now. The *Clarinet Quintet*. That's why I wanted to come in in the first place."

So Czeslaw fetched another stool and chair from the bar, set them up before the range for his unexpected colleague. And with that this bizarre chamber group of two set forth in the deserted kitchen of *The Red Boar Hotel* in the early morning of the winter solstice, 1952, on a journey that would take one of them back to heady days years earlier. You supplying the string reinforcements for your breakfast chef's clarinet; a duet lending dignity to the *Red Boar* hitherto quite unknown.

But nobody else had heard. Nobody else would ever know. And then after. Your new Polish friend had asked; "Goodness, you must have played that before."

"Yes."

"And that instrument – is it old? It looks very used, if that's the right word."

"Couple of hundred years."

"Christ, and it still works. Where's that from then?"

"Cremona, originally, but it's not as exotic as it sounds – there were lots of luthiers in northern Italy around at that time. Not to mention a few Germans, eager to learn from their reputation, who had crossed The Pyrenees to join them."

"Goodness me. Italian. We came through north Italy on our pilgrimage from Europe, a very far cry from direct of course, but a lot safer at the time. Where did you last use that then?"

"London."

Wiping up the cooking oil from the floor and cleaning the mouthpiece with the same grimy tea towel; "London. Goodness me, somewhere interesting no doubt?"

"The Royal Albert Hall."

By nine Czeslaw's private world was lost to the street bustle as he'd unlocked the front door.

51

And you?

Well... you'd faded, having no relish for seeing that rare dignity extinguished by a couple of residents booking in from Milton Keynes for a mid-winter break.

Back to your flat round the corner. Alone with your heady memories, including that of your new friend, who had had the envious privilege of walking amongst the ghosts of the very artisans who had built your instrument. Even – if it had just been en-route to a safer place.

Author's note.

I am only too well aware that all personnel working at Bletchley Park during the war took a fifty year oath of secrecy. Any breach of this would be breaking the Official Secrets Act – the breach in my story is only to serve narrative clarity. The oblique reference to Enigma *is true. The "electronic computer" called* Colossus, *was the first computer in the world and occupied the entire wall of a good sized room, and wasn't a small fraction as powerful as our current mobile phones. Alan Turing was of course a key figure at Bletchley and his electronic legacy we would all be completely lost without. Somewhat eccentric, Turing was in good company at Bletchley, but a little personal catastrophe is not so well known. He had inherited a collection of silver from his family, worth a considerable sum of money and in the interests of security he decided to bury it in some spot quite near Bletchley with the intention of retrieving it after the war. When Bletchley dispersed and Turing returned for the planned silver retrieval, he was horrified to find the foundations of Milton Keynes half-built over the burial site. His inheritance still lies beneath some dreary London commuter.*

Furthermore it should never be forgotten that when Turing was tried for homosexuality, then illegal of course, just after the war and found guilty, he was treated by chemical castration and his resulting suicide followed shortly afterwards. The great tragedy was that his defence lawyers, due to the fifty year Bletchley secrecy oath, were denied all knowledge of his wartime cracking of the German Enigma code which saved countless thousands of lives. It has always been the collective opinion of informed commentators ever since, that this shortened the war by about two years. The Queen granted him a posthumous Royal Pardon in December 2013.

Trump

letters@independent.co.uk, 9/12/15,
emailed: 4 PM, 9/12/15.

Sir or Madam,

Quoting from your editorial of yesterday: "…[Donald J Trump]. He is a buffoon on a global scale, yes, but…"

Well yes – a very nice satellite viewpoint with which probably most would agree, but a little snag – we want more.

So? In my dreams, I would write something along the following lines; "Dear Prime Minister, please would you formally invite Donald J Trump to spend a week free-ranging, disseminating his views throughout our country. *At the same time* I would also have written to you asking that you instruct all your political journalists and commentators to starve (intellectually) for the preceding week, depriving them of their staple diet.

Then, *and only then*, offering them what would effectively be Sunday lunch with all the trimmings at Claridges. The phrase "at their wits' end" springs to mind because it's their wit that is invariably their salt and pepper for even the most serious of matters, and with Trump they would have a field day, rather more, stalking and reporting to us for the duration of 'The Trump Tour'. I feel that perhaps for the first time ever, their wit might be threatened with running out, and that would be saying something.

In the highly unlikely event of of Donald J Trump making it to the White House, it would prove the cliché: 'money can buy anything' *and furthermore* it might even have put that same House on the same level as climate change, only for all the wrong reasons.

Dr Richard Wood,
Yorkshire.

"Demon Barber" slashed neck but spared jail

Daily Mirror, 24/10/14.

The hairdresser who used to run a shop called "The Demon Barber" walked free from court after slashing a man's neck with a cut-throat razor in a furious street row outside.

Lloyd Dobrodumow, 45, attacked Robert Charles Smith, 20, after an argument broke out in front of his shop, leaving him with a 10 cm (3.9 inch) wound to his throat.

Dobrodumow had been attempting to shut the door of his shop, "Jack's Salon", in Newcastle upon Tyne, when a scuffle broke out between the two men.

At the time of the incident, Mr Smith was carrying a plastic bag with alcohol in it, and was drinking from a can. When he had finished the can he tossed it away and then heard a male voice behind him saying "the bin is only f***ing there."

An argument then broke out between the two men and various witnesses saw Dobrodumow trying to close the door of his shop but Mr Smith placed his foot in the door.

Dobrodumow came out of his shop and witnesses saw Mr Smith swing the bag of lager at him. Dobrodumow then punched him in the face across his jaw – but with a razor in his hand.

Mr Smith was left with a 10-cm gash across his neck and blood began to soak into his T-shirt.

Witnesses then heard him demanding £10,000 from the defendant to "make it all go away", Newcastle crown court heard.

Mr Smith was taken to hospital following the incident, which happened at around 5pm on June 10 this year.

Dobrodumow had a long history of domestic violence and had 17 previous convictions.

Newcastle Crown Court: Toby Hedworth QC, mitigating, said he had suffered a series of incidents of anti-social behaviour outside his shop and was at the "end of his tether."

The defendant had shown "genuine tearful remorse", while witnesses had heard Mr Smith threatening to kill him, steal his dog and call his wife a slut.

Judge Tom Little accepted there had been no intent as Dobrodumow did not realise the blade was still in his hand as he used it every day at work.

"I have agonised long and hard about this decision and I'm just persuaded to suspend the sentence," he said.

The defendant admitted unlawful wounding on the basis that he had forgotten that he had had the razor in his hand during the attack.

He was given a 12 month suspended sentence, a 12 month supervision requirement with 200 hours of unpaid work, and ordered to pay £5,000 compensation, with £700 costs.

Police bike stolen, thief falls off

Northern Echo, 31/10/14.

A drunken man, Shaun Maher, bought ten pounds worth of cannabis together with the Durham Chief Constable's stolen bike who he claimed he had paid a man £60 for it, a court heard, and was found guilty at Peterlee Magistrates Court. He tried to pedal home but fell off Mike Barton's £650 hybrid machine in the street, knocking himself unconscious. The 32-year-old came round to find three men standing over him who told him they had called an ambulance. Fearing they might attack him, he "rode off on the blue and white bike to hide", he said. "But Maher was later arrested by police after being found slumped against a parked car in a drunken state", said John McGlone, prosecuting. "They spotted the bike nearby and Maher told officers it was his, and that he had bought it for £60 in Glasgow."

"He was arrested on suspicion of theft", said Mr Mc-Glone. "The bike was checked and a security number found on it revealed it to be missing from Mr Barton's home address." The hybrid bike, which had been secured to a bike rack, was stolen while the Chief Constable was on holiday. McGlone said Maher, of High View, Ushaw Moor, said he got it from a man he declined to name as he'd bought £10's worth of cannabis in Spennymoor on Sunday May 25th.

He was later arrested with the bike after police were called to reports of a drunken man in Hill View, Durham, at around midnight. PC Alistair Coulson said Maher seemed intoxicated.

Maher, who denied a charge of handling stolen goods, told Peterlee magistrates; "I was confused when I was arrested. I bought £10 of cannabis and he also gave me two white tablets which I took. He had a bike which I thought I'd seen him with before. He asked if I wanted to buy it. I didn't think it had been stolen and paid £60 for it."

The bench found the case proved, and fined him £160 together with £300 prosecution costs and a £20 victim surcharge.

Price of Christmas dinner slashed by stores

The Sun, 16/11/14.

The cost of Christmas dinner is now at its lowest since 2009, thanks to Lidl and Aldi.

The price of the festive basket is down three per cent from last year, meaning it will be possible to feed eight on the big day from as little as £2.66 each.

Good Housekeeping produced its cheapest Christmas dinner by comparing price tags across all 10 leading supermarkets.

And with chains such as Aldi and Lidl driving down costs, experts found this year's Christmas dinner is the third cheapest since 2009.

It means those who have volunteered to cook on Christmas Day could feed eight people for £21.31.

Good Housekeeping's Caroline Bloor said: "It's a constant struggle for many to keep family food bills under control.

"But the current battle between the supermarkets is pulling down prices for everyone – and will continue to do so.

"Even at the most expensive supermarkets there are still bargains to be found.

"The cost of potatoes and carrots is broadly the same across all retailers.

"It's a real time of change and we'll be monitoring it closely to see who is really focused on the customer."

The £2.66 Christmas dinner features a £9.99 turkey from Lidl, 49p sprouts from Aldi and £1.50 potatoes from the Co-op.

The cheapest one-stop shop was Iceland, Good Housekeeping found – with a dinner for eight people costing £27.84, including fresh vegetables. Last year's winner Lidl was second at £28.13.

No shred of wit in Jericho

feedback@radiotimes.com, ITV, Thursday 7th January, 9pm.

Dear Sir or Madam,

What a field-day could be had with Jericho. But no. I think script writer Steve Thompson (Sherlock, Doctor Who) here displays complete failure on every count. The field-day? The building of a viaduct in North Yorkshire's

Dales in the 1870s. Sanitising would be the understatement of the year.

The chat contains not a single shred of wit. No quick coarse repartee, the hallmark of such workmens' dialogue. The various wooden structures appear to be of timber direct from a modern builders' merchant, which perhaps it is, but does it really need to be so obvious?

The unwary viewer could be forgiven for thinking that the legendary bridge-builder Brunel's quite recent death had led somehow to his and his workforce's, complete replacement by the predecessors of Lord Grantham and his staff of Downton Abbey. At this rather earlier time the cleaners, butlers, waiters and gardeners were very poor navvies. Lord Grantham, his engineering colleagues and their wives' beautiful dresses and elaborate outfits hinted at Savile Row and Knightsbridge. And the navvies themselves – working on the viaduct's foundations – mud, filth, dirt and torn overalls? or had they just come off Downton's croquet lawn? But perhaps most extraordinary of all your viewer couldn't help but notice – never once a single coarse oath as they built the viaduct – very odd – unheard of in such a context.

If there was such a thing as a 'reality' grading system Jerico would score zero. I feel that here is a golden opportunity for a masterpiece completely missed.

Dr Richard Wood, Yorkshire.

"Gangster's moll" jailed

Daily Express, 13/10/14.

A glamorous blonde was branded as a "gangster's moll" by a judge who jailed her today for paying for her luxury wedding from her husband's crimes.

Bride Natasha Hugh, 27, spent almost £40,000 on her plush wedding to a former heavyweight champion boxer turned international cocaine dealer.

A court heard how beautician Hugh spent lavishly on luxury bridal wear – and an opulent wedding ceremony with chocolate fountains and casino tables.

The majority of transactions were dealt with in cash instalments – Mrs Hugh knew, or should have known, that the money had come from crime.

The mother-of-two and her drug-dealing husband then flew off on a dream honeymoon to Barbados.

Her extravagant lifestyle came to an end when 29-year-old former Welsh light-heavyweight champion boxer Justyn Hugh was jailed for running an international cocaine ring.

Hugh was found guilty of eight charges of laundering nearly £70,000 of her husband's £500,000 drug operation.

Prosecutor Roger Griffiths said: "Staff at the luxury hotel reception saw her paying a hairdresser from a 'blue gym bag' bulging with bank notes. There was a lavish life-style which wasn't sustainable on the declared earnings of Mr and Mrs Hugh. The majority of transactions were dealt with in cash instalments – Mrs Hugh knew, or should have known, that the money had come from crime."

Hugh splashed thousands of pounds in her home town of Newport, South Wales, during a four year spending spree.

Husband Justyn Hugh dealt drugs to fund his wife's extravagant lifestyle. A court heard she had a £10,477 wedding at the Vale Resort – a luxury four star golf, spa and leisure hotel near Cardiff as well as £2,260 on dental work and £2,435 on bridal wear and accessories, ahead of her plush ceremony.

Hugh also paid for a £3,900 holiday to Barbados using cash, staying at the Almond Causarina hotel on the Caribbean island as well as a Mini Sytner with almost £5,000 paid in cash, later exchanging it for a £19,570 Mini Countryman. After that £4,000 on hairdressing equipment for a beauty salon she set up called Glamorous U.

Cardiff Crown Court heard how she also spent £13,000 putting her child in nursery.

Hugh claimed her husband had a "controlling and violent nature."

TV soaps promote NHS time wasting

letters@independent.co.uk, 17/3/15.

From forty years experience as a GP, I write to heavily endorse Mary Leedham-Green's letter of yesterday. With the general election lurking, one of its fulcrums is our gold-dust NHS. And who collectively find themselves whether they like it or not, in a very strong position of influence? The script writers of our heavily watched TV soaps.

One such programme viewed by millions currently provides a shining example through a middle-aged woman, her family, and especially their young children. Typically; a simple domestic graze on the elbow, a finger cut in the kitchen from a ceramic knife – blood all over the floor. Goodness, all it needs is a spirit-dipped wipe, kitchen role with a dab of antiseptic, whisky even and a bit of sticking plaster, but oh no… "dear, dear darling – take her straight round to 'doctor' or A&E." Well surprise surprise; 'doctor' didn't spend seven years training for applying a sticking plaster. The soaps do offer their writers an opportunity to help (or otherwise). Their characters do, to some extent set an example to their viewers, particularly young ones.

So let those characters demonstrate at least some self responsibility; cutting your thumb off while using your

your table saw when your sister tripped and fell against you by accident is good reason to fly off to A&E. Banging your thumb hanging a photo on the wall is not.

The message is very simple – script writers please note.
If you want a National Health Service don't waste its time.

Dr Richard Wood, North Yorkshire.

God on the phone

To a lady friend who, unknown to me, had been a vicar, (my language leaving a lot to be desired)…

Dear ***,

I have to tell you a quick tale, bearing in mind that as we're working together you must't mind my language – (I'm sure you couldn't care less but it would not be respectful if I didn't at least mention it).

Anyway I had a patient (long dead now) who was our local Parish priest during the 1990s in Hinderwell. Over time we became quite good friends – I'd from time to time drop into the rectory, mid-day, for a couple of sherries with him and his wife. So in our family – three children – he was just called God.

He would occasionally have reason to phone me (not usually medical) and if Suzanna (10 yrs old) happen to answer she'd just shout "…God on the phone for you dad…" and we could hear him roaring with laughter in the background…

the best R.

Daughter charged with stealing from mother

The Times News, 31/10/14.

A Nesquehoning woman has been charged with stealing jewelry from her mother.

Nesquehoning police said Nicole Irene Canzoneri, 38, of 101 W. Diaz Ave., has been charged with theft and receiving stolen property.

She is also facing drug charges as a result of a search of her residence related to her arrest on the theft charges.

Borough police served a felony arrest warrant on Canzoneri on Thursday. A consent search was made of the residence and found drugs and drug paraphernalia including one spoon with resin, 10 baggies of heroin and pills.

Canzoneri was arraigned before District Judge Casimir Kosciolek of Lansford and committed to the county prison after failing to post $3,000 straight cash bail.

The investigation of the theft began on Oct. 23 when Chief Sean Smith received a call from the suspect's mother in reference to her Jeep being entered while parked at her home and jewelry being removed. The victim told Smith she was keeping the jewelry in her Jeep because she noticed, over the past few months, jewelry and money missing from her home.

Taken from the Jeep were various pieces of jewelry with an estimated value of $5,000.

The victim said she lived at the residence with her two daughters. Smith said there was no forced entry to the Jeep and that the victim said she kept one set of keys with her but a second set was missing from the residence.

Canzoneri was questioned about the incidents but denied any knowledge of the thefts.

On Oct. 24 Smith checked the Northeast Precious Metals database and discovered that Canzoneri was at the Time

Will Tell Pawn Shop in Lehighton on Oct. 24 and sold a 14 carat gold ring with pink stones, which matched one of the items stolen.

Through the course of the investigation Smith learned that Canzoneri had been at the Lehighton business on other occasions selling jewelry.

Video surveillance showed her selling the items and the business owner produced sales slips with her signature on them. This information led to the arrest warrant, which was served on the defendant.

Officer Timothy Wuttke assisted in the investigation.

Men who are victims of women's violence

Daily Mail, 31/10/14.

A woman who attacked her boyfriend with a hammer, pole and broken bottle was jailed for eight years after one of the worst cases of domestic violence police have seen.

Gemma Hollings, 37, attacked her partner after a row over hair straighteners. Paul Kirkpatrick, 30, was slashed across the neck with a broken bottle, and also hit with a hammer and pole leaving him with a broken bone in his face. Police found the victim covered in blood in the street after he ran from home. She was jailed for two counts of grievous bodily harm, and two of assault, in one of the worst cases of domestic violence police had ever seen. He told officers that she had caused the wounds after an argument over her hair straighteners.

Speaking after the hearing at Preston Crown Court, DC Jenny Berry said "The victim suffered very traumatic injuries. They could have potentially been fatal. This was a nasty attack. It is certainly one of the most serious cases of domestic violence I have ever come across. It was a relentless assault. Justice has now been done for the victim and he just wants to forget about the whole thing and move on with his life." She added "The bottle had been used to cause the injury to his neck. When the victim was found, he did not really understand the significance of his injuries. Since the attack, he has been able to move on. He has moved away and is not living in Darwen anymore. He has made a fresh start now that Hollings is in prison and the further away from her he is the better."

The officer said cases of domestic violence against men were not reported to police as often as those against women. She added "We do not hear of many cases of domestic violence against men because they are very much under-reported. This is the first domestic violence case I have dealt with which has involved a man. Tackling the issue is one of our main priorities and I would urge anyone, male of female, who is experiencing it to come forward."

Wendy Chappell, senior prosecutor, said "Gemma Hollings carried out a series of violent attacks on her partner over two days using her bare hands and several weapons.

He received extremely serious injuries resulting in him requiring hospital treatment. Everyone has the right to feel safe and be safe in their personal relationships, therefore, the CPS and police take all cases of domestic violence extremely seriously regardless of whether the victim is male or female. Bringing the perpetrators of such offences to justice remains a high priority.

Male domestic violence victims

Domestic violence is still a largely hidden crime, and police forces have been criticised for poor data collection on the issue. But based on current estimates, it is believed that 30 per cent of women and 16 per cent of men have experienced domestic abuse since the age of 16. Almost 40 per cent of domestic violence victims are thought to be male, with an estimated 720,000 men attacked in the last year, compared to 1.2million women.

That gap narrows considerably when it comes to the most severe type of abuse, with 1 per cent of men falling into that category, compared with 1.4 per cent of women.

While the issue is now more widely reported by all victims, men are still twice as likely to stay silent after abuse.

This year Home Secretary Theresa May raised the prospect of a new offence of domestic abuse. The new charge would cover grey areas such as stalking and financial control that are not wholly covered under existing laws.

Data provided by charity *ManKind*.

"I would like to encourage anyone who has been a victim of such offences to come forward and report it to the police and we will support you in every possible way."

Rachel Horman, a solicitor specialising in domestic violence, at Watson Ramsbottom, said men often felt too embarrassed to tell the authorities. She said "It is harder for men to come forward because of ideas of masculinity and that men should be tough. Some men feel ashamed, but I would urge them to get help from the police or domestic violence charities. They should not be embarrassed because every specialist will have dealt with men before."

According to Home Office statistics, 2.7 million men have experienced some form of domestic abuse in their lifetimes, with 700,000 victims reported in 2012/13 alone. A spokeswoman from the Hyndburn and Ribble Valley Domestic Violence Team said they often saw cases of domestic violence against men, but that there were still more women who came forward. She said "Regardless of gender, if you are feeling frightened or want someone to talk to about something going on in the home, give us a call and we can support you. Gender does not matter, everybody is treated as an individual."

Clive Grunshaw, Lancashire's police and crime commissioner said "Domestic abuse is a problem which affects all sections of society, and is one which I take very seriously. It is vitally important all victims – whether they are male or female – feel they are able to come forward. The courage and bravery displayed by the victim in this case is to be commended. Abuse is never the fault of the victim."

Does a girl have to be pretty for science?

The Guardian, 31/10/14.

"How pretty do you have to be to work on a building site?" Dressed to drill: what message does this hoarding on a Manchester hotel send out about women in the workplace? The picture is on the hoarding of The Malmaison Hotel, Manchester.

Jeanette Winterson: "One of my roles in life is professor of new writing at the University of Manchester. Last week I was given an honorary doctorate, along with Dame Julia King, vice-chancellor of Aston University, previously principal of the engineering faculty at Imperial College, London, after a distinguished career with Rolls-Royce.

We were discussing why more women don't go into engineering or applied science. The vice-chancellor of Manchester University, Dame Nancy Rothwell, is a physiologist, a director of AstraZeneca, and co-chair of the Council for Science and Technology. Both women agreed there is an 'image gap'. Women don't see themselves as practical scientists – even when they enjoy science and maths. And there are still so few role models out there.

Manchester is a university strong in the sciences – we have 25 Nobel Prize winners. And Manchester has always been a theory-into-practice kind of a place – that's why the Industrial Revolution started here. So if anywhere in the UK can encourage women into traditionally male-dominated professions, skills and research, then it is Manchester.

So imagine my outrage when I turned up in the city this week, and fronting the Malmaison, the hotel where I usually stay, is the hoarding in the picture. "Mal at Work" says the text. Women at work seems to mean wearing a strapless dress and full makeup while staring longingly at a drill that presumably doubles as a vibrator. I am not sure what the model intends to do with the spanner in another picture – undo something? A zip or a bolt?

Plenty of women on business stay at the Mal. To get to their hotel room at the end of a long day they must take in, or blank out, the message that women at work are really soft-porn babes.

And let's say you are a student studying engineering, or a PhD candidate doing research into the stress-load of materials. You've been out with your classmates – mostly, if not all, men – and you walk past the hoarding. Do you feel that engineering or construction offers a future where you will be treated equally? Will you look good in your hard hat? How much makeup should you wear on site? And anyway, aren't you just a pointy-headed version of Miley Cyrus on a wrecking ball?

Suppose you are a girl who wants to go into the manual trades? Electrician, plumber, site foreman, whatever. Does the image of a skinny model in a strapless frock, pouting with a spanner, do anything for your self-confidence and ambition? How pretty do you have to be to work on a building site?

When you put on your overalls in the morning is the first question you need to ask: "Does my bum look big in this?"

Everyday Sexism is running a campaign right now to educate the media, advertisers, schools and employers, in the problems around women and girls being bombarded with negative and conflicting mixed messages about sexuality and gender roles.

There is a photo of a man in a hard hat round the corner at the Mal. He's all muscle and sweat. He's a hunk, sure, but the visual message he offers is not confusing to men. He's about power and prowess, muscle and machismo. The hard-hat babes send out a message that aligns with male fantasy not female reality. And that's a problem.

Feminism is supposed to have triumphed. Women are supposed to be equal, yet the pay gap is widening. Reported incidents of rape and domestic violence are rising and women are not getting to the top of their professions. Anorexia and self-harm are increasing, and when we talk about sexual abuse, largely we are talking about men abusing women and girls. This week it was reported that prostitution added more than £5 billion to the economy in 2013. What kind of a world is this?

I conducted a quick straw poll outside the hotel yesterday. Some taxi drivers, parked opposite, liked the hoarding. A few people said they didn't notice it because the images are 'normal'. Some thought it was a joke.

Maybe it is a joke. The joke is that as Britain falls down the equality ladder behind Rwanda and Nicaragua, and Victoria Beckham is named entrepreneur of the year for dressing us all in size zero – some great clothes, but the same skinny models, the same skinny message – the nearest most women will get to being on the board is a strapless dress and a hard hat outside Malmaison."

Janner, Establishment and cattle prod

letters@independent.co.uk, *17/04/15*.

Sir,

The decision by The Crown Prosecution Service not to bring Labour peer and alleged multiple paedophile Lord Janner to trial is nothing short of pathetic. Why? As has been pointed out on several occasions, many people have been tried while in their nineties, war criminals have often been tried and prosecuted in absentia, so presumably their defence has functioned likewise.

You'd have thought Jimmy Saville would have been a wake-up call but, oh no, the duvet hasn't shifted an inch.

A satellite view currently shows our parliament and Justice system hovering above its nadir; Lord Janner will apparently remain a member of the House of Lords for life. Does The Establishment honestly expect the British public to take it seriously? What The Establishment really needs is a cattle prod up its bottom.

Dr Richard Wood.

War Book commended

feedback@radiotimes.com emailed 11/8/15, 10.45am.

War Book, BBC4, Tuesday 11th August 2015, 10am.

Dear Sir or Madam,

What a masterpiece – on every front.

First – the choice of conflict itself – perfect. The long term total sectarian ever-changing chaos rules out The Middle East. Anything involving China, Russia and America is far too obvious. India and Pakistan has been a nuclear tinderbox for a long time, begging for such treatment.

The acting was immaculate in itself, but furthermore utterly appropriate for each of their specific political roles – that's clever. Also none of the actors (with the possible exception of Shaun Evans, Endeavour), are especially well known and that always works well.

Finally not one but two vital ingredients missed on nearly all dramas. Constant wit along with realistic dialogue. Lawyers, doctors and politicians swear just as much and just as crudely as lorry drivers (no disrespect) and if anybody thinks otherwise it's high time they grew up. That was the most refreshing of all.

Dr Richard Wood.

Lawyers: how they build their reputation

The Sun, 28/10/14.

High profile lawyers in the United States of America make frequent appearances on national and international television. Criminal defence attorneys often seek some air time on major news channels that have a widespread audience base. The goal of such legal professionals is to shine some light on important issues that might be misunderstood by the public. Prominent criminal defence lawyers enjoy engaging in live interviews that might ask lots of tough questions. For example, some criminal defence attorneys may be harassed for defending certain celebrities who are sued in cases involving domestic violence or tax fraud.

Sometimes, high profile legal experts try to emphasise that their clients are on "witch trials" because of negative publicity generated by the mainstream media. It's common for major news outlets to sway public opinion about pending cases involving movie stars, politicians, athletes and entertainers. During on-going legal cases involving celebrities, lawyers usually handle most public relations issues in order to prevent any statements from being used out of context.

Some lawyers enjoy appearing on national TV shows that discuss general legal issues such as immigration, gang violence, gun control, white collar crime and more. After all, the average TV viewer is most likely unaware of legal codes that regulate such concerns. High profile attorneys believe that they have a responsibility to inform the public about issues that truly matter on a local or personal level.

True seekers of justice and order in the legal world are also quite active in the political arena. Some attorneys try to propose new legislation on municipal, state and federal levels. It's even possible for lawyers to offer their legal advice at major hearings that are held in the District of Columbia. Testifying in front of the United States Congress is truly an honour for a licensed lawyer who wants to change the legal system on a small scale.

High profile attorneys can also speak their minds on the radio. There are satellite and digital radio channels entirely dedicated to covering the latest legal issues. Prominent attorneys can provide their expertise and insight on some trending stories and other current events. Instead of listening to mainstream news outlets, many ordinary folks prefer to listen to "underground" radio stations that might discuss legal cases more openly. For example, lawyers might not be too concerned about political correctness when talking on a radio station that is heard by a small group of regional followers.

Social media is another powerful platform that can be used by high profile attorneys. Professional webpages can be created in order to advertise one's legal practice. Resumes can be uploaded for the entire world to see. Photos and videos might also enhance the online reputation of an attorney. For example, Joe Tacopina is a licensed attorney who uses social media for personal and professional networking.

Last but not least, attorneys who want to boost their reputation should connect with local people. It's important to appear in front of the public during events such as demonstrations, festivals and other large gatherings. Similarly, attorneys may also be invited as guest speakers at law school graduation ceremonies.

"Putin is destroying Russia"

The Guardian, 17/10/14.

"Putin is destroying Russia. Why base his regime on corruption?" asks Navalny. Russia's opposition leader and anti-corruption campaigner held under house arrest, says "President Putin is using war to stay in power."

Alexei Navalny at an opposition rally in Moscow, despite smears and little campaigning, won 27 percent of the vote in the mayoral elections. High in a dilapidated Soviet-era tower-block miles from the centre of Moscow, the door opens to a small, tidy flat. It belongs to Alexei Navalny, once touted as the most potent threat to the Russian president to emerge in recent years.

Since February, the politician and activist has been under house arrest. A voracious social-media user with a talent for 140-character attacks on the Kremlin, the 38-year-old is banned from using the telephone or internet, though his wife can use them. He only leaves the confines of his flat when a police van drives him to hearings of his latest court case.

In a recent relaxation of the terms of his arrest, he is now allowed to speak to people other than his relatives, meaning that for the first time in six months, his colleagues and friends can visit him. He is also able to receive journalists, and *The Guardian* is the first of the international press to see him since his house arrest began.

Dressed in a blue T-shirt and jeans, he pads barefoot through the small flat into the kitchen, where his wife, Yulia, pours tea. A tagging bracelet around his ankle ensures that if he leaves the flat the police will be alerted immediately.

"I'm really sick of sitting at home", he says, with a wry smile. In the corner of the living room is a cross trainer, the only way he can get exercise. "But I've had experience of real arrest for up to 15 days several times, and it's much easier to put up with house arrest when you understand what the alternative is."

Navalny was the great hope of the wave of street protests that shook Moscow in 2011-2012, with many opposition-minded Russians confidently predicting he would become the next president of Russia.

Those protests petered out after a vicious crackdown saw court cases against its leaders and some ordinary protesters, but Navalny is still the most worrying opposition figure for the Kremlin. Some uneasy liberals point to his nationalist streak and see in him a charismatic but dangerous demagogue.

What is clear is that he is able to win support among voters. Despite smears on state television and little access to any normal type of campaigning, he managed to win 27 percent of the vote in last autumn's Moscow mayoral elections.

Since then, a lot has happened, notably the annexation of Crimea and the fighting in east Ukraine. A summit in Milan on Friday attended by Putin, Ukraine's president Petro Poroshenko, and other European leaders including the German chancellor Angela Merkel, failed to reinforce the faltering ceasefire.

Despite the fact that many Russian nationalists support the separatists in east Ukraine, Navalny feels Putin has laid the groundwork for his regime's eventual collapse.

"There's a lot of commentary now that Putin has shown he's not about money, enriching his businessmen buddies or to resurrect the Soviet Union, but has decided to build a great nation, a great Russia", says Navalny, who first became known for his anti-corruption investigations, unveiling the secret mansions and foreign accounts of Putin cronies and government officials. "I think in reality it's all much simpler. Putin has resorted to the method that various leaders have used for centuries; using war or military actions to solve internal problems and boost ratings. That happens even in democratic countries – look at Bill Clinton in Yugoslavia."

Unlike most of the liberal opposition, who have never found a common language with ordinary Russians, there was always a sense in the Kremlin that Navalny could be dangerous; a fear that his nationalism and charisma could appeal not only to the Moscow hipsters, but equally to the provincial masses, tired of seeing rampant corruption blight the country's governance.

Those in power have long been split about how to deal with the troublesome campaigner; some believe he should be locked up, others think he should be free but closely monitored. For a while in 2013, it looked as if an allegation of embezzling funds from a timber company in the city of Kirov would put him in prison; but he was released after a surprise about-face, given a suspended sentence, and allowed to run in Moscow's mayoral elections.

His good showing there clearly spooked some of those in power. A second court case, based on claims that Navalny and his brother defrauded a Russian subsidiary of the French chain Yves Rocher, began. In February he was put under house arrest and the case has been rumbling on since.

The strategy for now seems to be to shut him up without causing too much of a scandal. To a large extent it has worked. There has been little outcry over the fact that he is under house arrest, after all he is not in jail. But at the same time, working on his anti-corruption investigations has become impossible, but largely disappeared from public discourse. With everything else happening in Russia, even the hearings of the second court case got just a fraction of the attention that the Kirov case received. Navalny says about 30 prosecution witnesses have been called so far, and "all of them ended up testifying in our favour – it's stupid and completely absurd."

He puts the strange zig-zagging in the case down to the fact that nobody lower down in the system knows what to do with him.

"Obviously it will be a guilty verdict, but what the sentence will be can only be decided by one man, and that man has a lot of stuff on his plate besides me at the moment. He's fighting a war against Obama, against the west, against God knows what else."

The authorities continue to keep Navalny on his toes, and there is always the threat of new criminal cases. Sometimes the charges appear so flimsy they veer into the realm of the absurd. Over the summer, his flat was raided by investigators who seized a picture. The picture had been drawn by a street artist in the town of Vladimir, and been on display on a public wall. Someone pilfered it and gave it to Navalny as a present. "The artist has given interviews everywhere saying he never sells his art, that he doesn't care that it was taken, that he doesn't want there to be a court case, but they just ignore him – the case exists. From the case materials we can see that FSB (security services) generals are working on the it; they have six top investigators working on it!" Employees of Navalny's anti-corruption foundation have been questioned, searches carried out, computers and telephones seized.

Indeed, Navalny is such a toxic figure in Russia that any association with him can lead to trouble. In the Kirov court case, a former business partner was hauled into the dock alongside the politician. His brother Oleg is also on trial in the current case. "That's one of the most unpleasant parts of my work, because everything that happens around me is basically one giant court case, which spreads out to engulf the people that are close to me", he says. It's been hinted at several times that he would be better off leaving the country, but he decided to stay. Is he really more use to the opposition cause under house arrest, or potentially in jail, than he would be from abroad? "Why should I leave? I have not committed any crime. You can agree or disagree with my political position but it's absolutely legal. And along with me, 90 percent of Russians think corruption is high, and 80 percent of Russians think we should bring criminal cases against corrupt officials. It's also an important matter of trust. If I want people to trust me, then I have to share the risks with them and stay here. How can I call on them to take part in protests and so on if they are risking things and I am not?"

He says it is pointless to make predictions either about his own fate or about how much longer Putin will be in power. Navalny has set up a political party, although it is not able to contest elections, and says he still harbours ambitions that one day he will be actively involved in politics, "including fighting for the top job."

As for how Putin will finally end up leaving the Kremlin – through a split in the elite, a violent revolution or a democratic transition – Navalny believes one thing is for certain; "In Russia, it will not be elections that provide a change of government."

Navalny in his own words:

On Mikhail Khodorkovsky, formerly owner of Yukos, Russia's biggest oil company, who was jailed in 2003, released in 2013 and now lives abroad:

"Perhaps if he had stayed an oligarch, I would have had a lot of points of dispute with him, particularly on the rights of minority shareholders, which I worked on as a lawyer. Yukos was famous for various corporate battles. But that was 10 years ago, and discussing it is pointless. I don't see any position that Khodorkovsky has now that I don't share."

On Putin's reaction to Ukraine:

"Out of nowhere, without any warning, boom. Suddenly a genuine, anti-criminal revolution. This was a terrible blow for Putin, a hundred times more painful than the Georgian events, than former president Mikheil Saakashvili and his anti-corruption reforms. He cannot allow this in Ukraine. So I think one of his strategic goals in the coming years will be to do absolutely everything to undermine the Ukrainian state, to ensure that no reforms work, so that everything ends in failure."

On the consequences of Russian actions in Ukraine:

"Putin likes to speak about the 'Russian world' but he is actually making it smaller. In Belarus, they sing anti-Putin songs at football stadiums; in Ukraine they simply hate us. In Ukraine now, there are no politicians who don't have extreme anti-Russian positions. Being anti-Russian is the key to success now in Ukraine, and that's our fault."

On what he would ask Putin:

"I would be interested to understand his motivations, particularly on Ukraine, because he is destroying our country. Surely he can't not understand that it's all going to collapse. If he wants to be an authoritarian leader, then that's one thing. But why doesn't he want to be a Russian Lee

Kuan Yew? Why does he want to base his authoritarian regime on corruption? There are other ways of doing it."

On finding the 'Putin account':

"I think there are probably a few numbered accounts in Swiss banks where money is kept that Putin considers his personal money. But in the main it is all kept by nominal holders, like head of Russian Railways, Vladimir Yakunin or the Rotenbergs, two billionaire brothers, who are childhood friends of Putin. The money is communal. If intelligence services really wanted to find Putin's money there would be ways of doing so, but all we can do is work with open sources and the information we get from insiders. We can't show up at a Swiss bank and seize documents or analyse transfers. Corruption in Russia is so open that even we can find a huge amount. But to find Putin's accounts, that's beyond our capabilities."

On how he spends his time under house arrest:

"I'm reading a huge number of books; basically doing what everyone dreams of doing but never has time for. I'm watching the '250 best films ever' one by one. All this American nonsense like *The Good, the Bad and the Ugly*, and other old films."

Atheism in education

to: pcu.correspondence@education.gsi.gov.uk, 12/1/12.

Dear Sir or Madam,

I speak as a near lifelong atheist, which I have been since the age of about eight. Originally it was lit and fuelled by an interest in World War II, not that it itself had much to do with religion, but prompted exploration on my part that did. My opinions were maintained thereafter by dissatisfaction with both arguments supporting, and behaviour by, religious denominations that I came into contact with either directly, through friends, books, the press, or the media in general. Currently The Middle East has of course much to answer for. Perhaps I should add here that am not a pacifist, and should it ever be required, I would play my part in whatever way was appropriate.

Religion has lurked beneath war since time immemorial; The Crusades being an early glittering example. They might be far better remembered by their inadvertent revelation of penicillin; mouldy bread slapped on their wounds speeded healing. They then would have earned the blue plaque on the side of one of their tents which has honoured Sir Alexander Flemming on the entrance arch of St Mary's Hospital, Paddington (where I trained) celebrating his 'discovery' of the drug in 1928.

All this gelled in my taking an early path towards science in general as an overall philosophy, culminating in my profession of medicine. But from much earlier, it has been my firm conviction that all, including the ether itself, have an origin requiring no deity of any kind. Our understanding might not have quite got there yet; just give us a little more time.

Travelling throughout Europe and a year working in East Africa showed me that religion has many faces, most of whom frown upon each other. The word that is italicised in my mind has always been hypocrisy of one kind or another.

Darwin made complete sense, and an atheist's view was scientifically sound, honest and peaceful; probably representing the peace antithesis to the war that all religions put together have represented since time began.

The point of all this is my question: why is the concept of atheism never put on the table to our children, as a belief as plausible a life's path to follow as any of the more conventional routes usually taught. This especially more so as it is highly likely nowadays in this country, that classes will comprise a multitude of culture, race and colour more than ever. Teaching atheism would be a problem because by definition, it would mean undermining all other religious followings, which would be completely destructive and counter-productive by anybody's book.

My point is simply to draw to the attention of our children that atheism is a creed that not only exists, but is followed by many of our most highly respected, and perhaps most important of all, when it comes to violence, its track record is no better or worse than anybody else's. Children are born areligious – that's semantically correct – and could usefully remain so until such time as they possess the wherewithal to make their own minds up, rather than being brainwashed from birth into whatever creed their parents follow.

At Harrow (named only because it's central to my point), we had to attend 'chapel' every morning for a short service (longer on Sundays). This took about twenty minutes.

My own views were of course by this time, well fused. I was fifteen, and made an appointment to see the head master, Dr James, a well respected, liked and highly civilised man. I quote, not verbatim obviously, but accurate spiritually (might sound dated, but that's how things were):

"Sir, thank you for agreeing to see me. I hope you will not mind my request."

"Wood (all surnames then of course), please go on."

"Well sir, it's that I'm a firm atheist, always have been. And I'm wondering if therefore I might be excused chapel, except Sundays, as it means absolutely nothing to me. I'm just wasting the Chaplin's time. I would do anything useful in that time, help the house staff – washing up, gardening, anything that you say. I must be able to help somebody."

"Well Wood, I do appreciate your request, and more importantly respect it. However there is a problem; this school was founded in 1571, and the founders, at the time, laid down a decree that all pupils must attend worship, every single day as well as Sunday. Moreover this decree must be adhered to for all time in the future (words to that effect), and must be enforced by the School Governors hereafter."

"You see, Wood, unfortunately my hands are tied. I respect your request and it does sound quite ridiculous that I'm tied by what was said 390 years ago, but unfortunately I am, and not just me but the School Governors also are tied."

And so that was that. I just took a novel in to chapel, and no one objected to that.

So I offer that as a salute to atheism, and a wish that it commanded more respect in our schools, and our Department of Education.

Richard Wood.

Atheism in schools

North Yorkshire County Council, 9th March, 2012.

Dr R Wood
Via email dr_dick@hotmail.co.uk

Dear Dr Wood,

Thank you for taking the time to share your views on atheism with me. I can see from your letter that you have thought long and hard about the big questions around creation and the different interpretations that individuals hold.

The law states that all pupils within state schools must study Religious Education. The form that Religious Education takes in our schools in North Yorkshire, as in other areas of England and Wales, is decided by a local statutory body, SACRE. This consists of volunteers representing major world faiths and local councillors. The role of the Local Authority is to advise, and not direct, this body. The present membership of North Yorkshire SACRE does include representation from non religious world views.

As you may be aware North Yorkshire's current 'Agreed Syllabus for Religious Education' does not specify non religious world views, such as atheism, as an area of study. However, it does not preclude non religious views either. The syllabus has to, by law, include the six major world religions with a focus on Christianity to reflect our historical and cultural heritage. However, schools can opt to include additional world views and many of them do as part of exploring big questions around issues like creation and suffering, both of which you refer to as factors contributing to your beliefs. Many other people still interpret the same issues in a religious way and we must respect all views. The present syllabus is concerned to help pupils develop an open, sensitive and reflective approach to understanding humankind's varied religious practices, values, beliefs and lifestyles, relating these to their own experiences and to questions of everyday life.

I am sure you will be interested to know that we are currently reviewing the syllabus and it is likely that SACRE will include the option to explore non-religious views and perspectives, alongside religious ones. This will reflect more accurately the diversity of religious and non-religious views in North Yorkshire and the country beyond.

As for Collective Worship, the 'Schools Standards and Framework Act', 1988, requires all maintained schools to provide a daily act of collective worship for all pupils, from which parents have the right to withdraw their children if they wish. In community schools, and foundation schools without a religious character, it must be wholly or mainly of a broadly Christian character. The aim of collective worship is to promote spiritual, moral and social development.

Yours sincerely,
***
Corporate Director – Children and Young People's Service.

End secrecy of confessional – Archbishop

The Times, Wednesday 22nd October, 2014.

Child abusers should no longer be protected from justice by the confidentiality of the confessional, the Archbishop of York told *The Times* today.

Dr John Sentamu said that after listening to survivors of sexual abuse by a senior clergyman he had pressed the Church of England to undertake legal and theological study on the secrecy of confession.

Under canon law priests are forbidden from disclosing what is said to them in the confessional. The Archbishop said: "Jesus said the greatest person in the kingdom is not the bishop or the priest, it's the child... I would rather stick with Jesus than stick with anything else."

Booze-fuelled strip on London Underground

London Evening Standard, 31/10/14.

A District Line tube train was taken out of service after members of London university's Imperial College rugby club apparently played a booze-fuelled stripping game on board. The group carrying kit bags and wearing their college rugby sweatshirts stripped bare and ran amok on the District Line train yesterday evening. According to commuters; 'They boarded towards the front of the 17.19 Richmond to Upminster service, swigging from bottles of wine'. At least one of them was said to have stripped naked on the platform at Richmond station and boarded the train.

They were apparently playing a game in which you had to get off the train, strip, and board again before it moved off. A witness, who did not want to be named, described their behaviour as 'disgraceful – total disregard was shown to fellow passengers'. The train was halted at Stamford Brook and everyone on board was told to disembark because of the disturbance.

A spokeswoman said: 'At around 5.30pm yesterday a train was held for about eight minutes at Stamford Brook station due to reports of a group of naked men on a District Line train between Richmond and Upminster.

It was then emptied of passengers, de-trained and The British Transport Police were called. We conducted a search of the area but did not find anyone matching the description'. Enquiries continue.

Imperial College said in a statement: 'The Students' Union has very clear policies and rules in place regarding the behaviour of all members of its clubs and societies'.

Stalin's atheism

letters@independent.co.uk, 24/1/15.

Dear Sir or Madam,

Yasmin Alibhai-Brown's book might be described as politically, religiously and socially reasonable from three hundred and sixty degrees. But what it and just about every text on her and related subjects, for interesting comparison, fails to mention is *atheism*.

Atheism holds a trump card to which every single religion or belief (with the exception of Buddhism – not a religion of course) has to bow.

In its own right atheism has never ever incited violence or war since man first developed the facility for cognitive thinking.

Stalin was atheist but that was entirely tangential to his politics.

Hitler was skeptical of religion altogether, though raised early as Catholic. Generally speaking any religious questions surrendered to his immediate political requirements, but he could never be described as atheist in the true sense.

I have for sixty years wondered how atheism has completely escaped mention in 'religious studies' throughout our education system. I have over time, been in communication with both Westminster and North Yorkshire Education Authority; neither offering the slightest useful reply. We are a multicultural society and the realms of particle physics offer, at the very least, as equal an answer as any deity.

Yours sincerely,
Dr Richard Wood.

Political boundaries torpedo local identity

The Sun, 22/10/14.

Matthew Engel's book details how local government reform contributed to the loss of our historic counties and regional identity in the North.

It was refreshing to hear someone born outside of the region have a good word to say about Ashington. He had more than a good word in fact. He admires the people who live there and what they represent.

Why? Identity. Engel, a writer for *The Guardian* newspaper for 25 years, sometime editor of the 'cricket bible' Wisden and now a columnist for *The Financial Times*, visited the Northumberland town while researching his latest book called Engel's England. He spent three years re-visiting the old counties which disappeared off the map of Britain as a result of the Local Government Act.

Drawn up by Ted Heath's Tory Government in 1972, it was implemented by Harold Wilson's Labour on, appropriately I would guess in Engel's mind, April 1st – April Fool's Day – 1974.

"It was a shambles", he said. "Politicians are interested in political boundaries. People are not. We don't care about local government and local government gets worse and worse, causing a huge loss of local identity, but there are still things left. Things to celebrate that really have an identity; Places like Ashington.

"What a tremendous place. Of course it has its problems but it has a tremendous richness of associative life. Associative life means a clearly identified way of life, from recognisable pass-times like growing leeks and racing whippets. Something that hasn't been lost despite the decimation of the coal mines in the area" he said. "It is a place with its own accent, it's own traditions, which are very, very strong."

In the book he explained how counties were formed historically and how they developed along locally defined lines which threw up their own idiosyncrasies. There were the counties palatine, including Durham, which were directly under the control of a local princeling.

Then there were counties corporate and boroughs that were regarded as self governing and fell under the control of the local Lord Lieutenant for military purposes. Yorkshire, readers may well remember, was divided into three ridings.

"As a result counties developed their own laws, dialects, customs, farming methods and building styles. They formed the tapestry of the nation", Engel says. "The very distinctions show just how important the county was in the lives of the people. Real places with real differences inspiring real loyalties."

The Local Government Act of 1888 brought democracy to the shires by establishing county councils but, according to Engel, the integrity of the counties was respected.

Not so; The Local Government Act of 1972 which binned centuries of local identity to see, for example, Teesside renamed as Cleveland and Tyneside becoming Tyne and Wear. Cumberland – which had been around since the 12th century – became part of Cumbria, a name that Engel shudders with distaste at; "always say Cumberland", he says.

Yarm had formed part of the Stokesley Rural District in what was then the 'North Riding' of Yorkshire and remained so until 1974, when it became part of the district of Stockton-on-Tees in the new non-metropolitan county of Cleveland. Cleveland – like Tyne and Wear – was abolished in 1996 under the Banham Review, with Stockton-on-Tees becoming a unitary authority.

In May a poll inspired by the Yarm for Yorkshire group saw locals vote emphatically "Yes" to the idea of transferring Yarm from Stockton to Hambleton Council in North Yorkshire. Last month Stockton Borough Council rejected calls to refer the matter to the boundary commission, but the debate rumbles on.

To add to the horror of Teessiders who pine for a return to Yorkshire was this bit of research from Engel after a talk with a dialect expert from Leeds University. "He told me Middlesbrough accents have actually changed in the years since 1974. In those 40 years the Middlesbrough accent has become more North East and less Yorkshire."

Engel describes his work as a "travel book." "I think I'm the first travel writer who went straight from Choral Evensong at Durham Cathedral to the dog track", adding; "The historic counties need to return to the map, the media and our envelopes so future generations can understand where they live. Only then will the English regain their spirit the way the Scots have. This is not about local government – it is about our heritage and our future."

Simon Raven (Part One)

(...or who could it be?)

At school I think I read just all that Evelyn Waugh had ever written. Wonderful, I thought at the time.

Later I was to change my mind.

I was a Senior House Officer – SHO – working at The Canadian Red Cross Memorial Hospital in Taplow, Buckinghamshire. Outside the ground-floor wards were corridors originally for TB patients to sit out in wheelchairs, good fresh air being a traditional part of the treatment. Nurses would take them out, as time aloud, for short walks around the flat grassy surroundings

Now five minutes walk up the road was a pub (for our purposes here) – *The Mole & Shovel*, a small un-fussy country pub, which didn't even do food beyond crisps and peanuts, but it did serve decent beer. I can't remember the brewery, but it certainly flew in the face of the disgusting Watney's Red Barrel which was horrifically sweeping the country at the time.

Now I had become great friends with a colleague by the name of Paul Kennedy, at the same stage as myself but in the Obs & Gynae department, the route he was to follow thereafter. And it became a habit after we'd finished our evening meal, to saunter up to *The Mole* for two or three pints and a good goss between ourselves, the landlord, and some of the locals whom we got quite friendly with.

Now I have to say that doctors are sitting targets for many people to strenuously try and bulldoze the ethic of patient confidentiality, more so in this situation if somewhat lubricated. but reassuringly for readers we never succumbed. The hospital was well aware of our habit, had the pub number and would occasionally phone if either of us was wanted. Such routine was entirely normal and had we

91

worked in any large hospital it would have taken us much the same time to reach a ward as it did for us to trot from the pub. As for alcohol I think two and a half pints was the most we ever had, usually just two.

Anyway on one such occasion Paul was already up there when I'd finished on the ward and when I arrived he was already sitting, trying to read despite badgering from other drinkers trying to elicit material that would do well for the front cover of a woman's magazine.

After getting my drink I joined him at one of the heavy small round cast-iron-legged tables. I can't remember the sort of things our dialogue usually followed, beyond the fact that contrary to what television would have you believe, it was never, ever about work. I can't speak for any other profession, but of doctors, when they go to the pub at night they enjoy themselves just like anybody else, and not yack on about their patients who they're delighted to be free from.

Putting my pint down firmly –

"So Paul what may I ask is that you're reading?"

"Well wouldn't you like to know?"

"That's why I'm asking."

Throughout my life I've read very little fiction, apart from the Evelyn Waugh phase as mentioned, and lots of H G Wells when much younger.

"I remember you saying you'd read lots of Evelyn Waugh stuff at some stage."

"Well yea, a while back. But don't read much fiction at all really."

"Well if you do decide to revert to it at anytime you'd do well to forget Waugh's Brideshead,, the Catholic church, frolicking about on the croquet lawn and get something a little more penetrating down your neck."

"Really. And penetrating just what might I ask?"

"Most that you can think of. Especially the middle and upper-middle classes, business people and financiers, whores, newspapers, journalism, seedy corrupt lawyers and not forgetting the privileged titled cream. In short just about any working community and social group that springs to mind is dismantled with exquisite wit, piercing cynicism and perhaps most unusual and unexpected realism. A large group of clever and not-so-clever people over a period of many years intimately dismantled with a literary scalpel and tweezers. And one prostitute serving many, yet practicing the ethics associated with the medical profession and she never slips up, not once. Try it. Waugh doesn't even get to what my American wife would call first base. Time you switched to someone little more sophisticated. Waugh wasn't particularly clever, just hovered about in circles he'd grown up with, then inflated by The Vatican. He was just a rather older Blue Peter – Children's 5 o'clock tele. Complete socially neolithic crap, so there you go. Grow up – join the real world.

"And what can you tell me is 'The Real World'.

Alms for Oblivion. Ten novels. They are sequential but in fact do stand up as individual stories and there is no need to read them in order, they are all cross-referenced as you go.

"And so who, as I asked you ten minutes ago?"

"Simon Raven. Read him Richard." So I did. Paul was quite right. I changed my mind.

Simon Raven (Part Two)

Evelyn Waugh was much constrained by his religious convictions – The Catholic Church constrained him somewhat but his writing largely reflects his middle to upperclass breeding and life style in general. Certainly he does tease his background, but only in a rather restrained way. Of course that must to some extent be a perfectly reasonable reflection of the life and times of the day in this country, but should him and Simon Raven share the sofa on say *Good Morning Britain,* I doubt whether Waugh would metaphorically get a word in edgeways.

Let me extract a tiny quote from one of Raven's main characters, Captain Detterling, from his novel *The Survivors,* published 39 years ago; he, Detterling, had become a marquess by an extraordinarily convoluted and unexpected route, and quote "…He had done with the House of Commons: he was not inclined to attend more than occasionally, the charade that was now The House of Lords. Although he would continue as an active partner with Gregory Stern, etcetera…"

There has of course recently been much discussion as to the very raison d'être of the unelected House of Lords, nearly forty years after just the same had obviously occurred to this perceptive novelist. I would describe Raven's immediately recognisable literary signature as effortlessly torpedoing our long accepted domestic architecture, usually in a single sentence, and inevitably upheld and emphasised by effortless wit. It's that which elevates it to the heights it commands.

A shining example of this whole issue occurred quite recently with Lord Janner*. Allegedly guilty of countless paedophilic sexual offences many years ago, he was excused trial on the grounds that he'd gone loco through Alzheimer's and thus unfit for trial. Despite this he was considered quite fit to remain in The House of Lords. Whoever was behind this train of thought must also have gone completely loco, and forgot that several Nazi war criminals were tried in absentia as they wallowed in bars, rat-arsed, in South America. As there was no extradition

94

treaty existent between this neck-of-the-woods and Europe, many of Hitler's regime rapidly emigrated as their war evaporated and failure became the inevitability.

As well as being widely documented, this scenario was brought home to me personally when I worked with a practice in East Sussex in 1977. I had a patient whose business had an office in Buenos Aeries, requiring a monthly trip to Argentina, involving a week's stay in the city. He needed to see me on a regular basis for a while, nothing very serious, but monthly blood checks were indicated for some weeks.

On learning all this I got my receptionist to book his appointments at the end of my evening surgery, usually somewhere around 6.30, and this would leave us time to chat, and indeed sometimes for drink on the way home at the near-by local pub. At such sessions he would tell me many tales of his south American business trips where in the evenings he along with colleagues, would visit a selection of bars and clubs often populated, as well as locals, by several ex-Nazis, by that time in their seventies and eighties.

They remained a tight-knit, self-supporting group, sharing the habit of excessive alcohol consumption, arrogance and the rowdy drunken singing of nationalist, crude Nazi songs. It also came to his notice through a variety of sources, that the Catholic Church there played a significant role in their early sponsorship, none of which was regarded as especially guarded knowledge as by this time these, to all intents and purposes, war criminals, had become well integrated citizens, with perfectly normal jobs.

But back to Simon Raven, our novelist, and held by myself as an interesting, and probably the most relevant, yardstick to which Waugh could (and usefully should) be held for comparison. Waugh's staple diet was the middle class, a choppy sea just above and just below which his head would would bob, but always allowing his free-range gut to digest his chosen facets as he pleased at their own expense, and without doubt to the huge enjoyment of his readership (of which I was one for some years).

Until I quite suddenly and completely changed my mind.

Simon Raven has written several works, easily checked through all the usual modern search techniques available easily to all. If that's all you need – easy. Do it. But should you want to show something off to someone who had made clear to you that her (yes a woman) had rather more of a voracious appetite for literary caviare supplemented by rich red Rioja. Then finalise thins by offering to drive her back to your small house in a side street off West-bourne Grove in your maroon Ford Cortina, find a little side street beside a small straggly grass square surrounded by trees. Then park. And then, and only then, gently pull her close with your left arm to whisper in her right ear; "now my dear come in and join me, one or two friends, and my wife of course, in some of the most delightful sexual proclivities that conventional pornography would not recognise if it stared them in the face." Could she seriously refuse? of course not.

Put in a nutshell; a series of ten novels, collectively called *Alms for Oblivion*, Raven completely dismantles just about all conventional faces of our national domestic system. Business, Politics, alcohol, sexual conventions, family relationships, along with what most consider to be a 'normal family structure', to the very seediest that otherwise straightforward folk might, unexpectedly and certainly unintentionally, might become if they fall out of control.

Think about all that for a bit and you might be getting somewhere near the (sorry for the cliché) page where Simon Raven lives.

RHW, January 2016.

* At the time I wrote to The Independent *(published) stating the above arguments about Lord Janner, and just recently after his death there is a move to get a "trial of facts" in an attempt to prove that there was truth in the allegations, thereby offering a degree of peace for his alleged victims' families.*

To the Alliance of Green Socialism local rep

8/5/15.

Dear Juliet,

I look forward to meeting you for tea and crumpets tomorrow pm. I have made a few comments in your published manifesto which we might chat about. In case you're interested (which you well might not be) I have several comments.

First I am not a politician, neither have I the slightest interest in politics. I am a scientist pure and simple. Science and logic fuelled by experience, dictate my every move.

Medicine respects nothing – race, social standing, colour, religion and, perhaps most of all, politics. Our (UK – notwithstanding Sturgeon) political flavour for each semi-decade of course does accede to the current political dictates over the NHS to a point. But frankly if you're a doctor on a ward round each morning, and in the ward office at noon discussing the multi-options of managing an unusual patient with a pancreatic-induced hypoglycaemia you really couldn't give a shit whether it's Cameron or Screaming Lord Such at the national helm. The one general exemption is perhaps that the constant changes that this parliament has insisted on dropping on us every five minutes for no perceptible clinical advantage is more than irritating. Mistress (much too feminine a word for the so called Iron Lady, who my profession prays rusts in Hell) Thatcher was the worst. Her funeral disgusted many, many people certainly me. The medical profession harbours considerably more intelligence than the Corpocracy put together and resents being interfered with by people whose 'brain' fuel is principally money. Mind you I have to admit that I have never met, let alone had a conversation with, a politician before, so lets just enjoy our crumpets. I was amazed that you knew Lindsay quite well, and you'll be pleased to know and I can pass on, that she speaks highly of you.

See you tomorrow, the best – Richard.

NHS doctor flees UK to join Taliban

The Telegraph, 16/11/14.

A British surgeon who was due to stand trial for assault has fled the country and become a senior leader of the Taliban in Pakistan.

Mirza Tariq Ali, 39, who practised in the NHS, evaded the UK authorities despite having his passport taken from him while awaiting trial at the Old Bailey.

He resurfaced last week in a recruitment video for a Taliban splinter group, urging foreign jihadists to join him. The doctor has become a mouthpiece for the terrorist organisation and under a new name — Dr Abu Obaidah Al-Islamabadi — has begun publishing an English-language jihadist magazine online, aimed at recruiting Muslim youths from the West.

Ali, who lived in Walthamstow, east London, arrived in Britain in 2004, having previously been a doctor in the Pakistan army. He worked shifts as a locum surgeon in London and Cambridge, having trained at a London teaching hospital.

Police and security services are now facing embarrassing questions over how he was able to flee. The surgeon is one of a growing number of known extremists who have skipped bail or surveillance to wage "holy war" abroad.

The Sunday Telegraph can also disclose that another man, a terrorist suspect believed to have been planning a suicide bomb plot abroad, fled the UK in recent months in the back of a lorry despite having his passport seized on the orders of the Home Secretary. The 26-year-old, of Somali origin and who lived a few streets from Ed Miliband, the Labour leader, in north London, had known associations with terror organisations dating back to 2008.

In the case of Ali, he had been held twice by police, and in November last year was briefly imprisoned for breaching his bail before evading the Metropolitan Police and MI5, then travelling abroad. He slipped out of Britain in an attempt to travel to Syria to join Islamic State of Iraq and the Levant (ISIL), according to his video, while awaiting his trial at the Old Bailey on a violent disorder charge.

He was sentenced in his absence in June this year to 15 months in jail.

Penguins liaising with seals

Mail Online, 18/11/14.

A new thing: scientists from the University of Pretoria regularly monitor wildlife on Marion Island for rare and unusual behaviour: *fur seals mating with penguins.*

Although the behaviour has been spotted once before, in 2006, this recent spate suggests the acts are becoming more widespread.

Each of the four recorded sexual incidents showed the seal chasing, capturing and mounting the penguins.

They then attempted to copulate for between two-and-a-half and six minutes before they are seen resting and trying again. The average copulation time was five minutes.

Experts suggest it may have become a learned behaviour, because the incidents have occurred with different fur seals. And the incidents may continue, but the reasons why the seals have started to exhibit it are not known.

The researchers speculated that the male seals may be sexually inexperienced, frustrated, or it may be an act of aggression. They may also have difficulty recognising female seal partners.

"Honestly I did not expect that follow up sightings of a similar nature to that of 2006 would ever be made, and certainly not on multiple occasions", Nico de Bruyn, of the Mammal Research Institute at the University of Pretoria, South Africa told the BBC.

"Determining the drivers of the unusual behaviour is nearly impossible", explained the researchers. "However we can only speculate as to what may have ultimately led to the sexual coercion of individuals from these very different species."

For example, Mr De Bruyn originally suggested, that the sexual coercion was a result of the seal's predatory behaviour towards the penguins being redirected into sexual arousal. A disturbing video shows a seal attempting to mate with a penguin. But in the light of a 2011 attack – when the seal killed the penguin – he added that this seems less plausible.

Another suggestion from experts is that the attacks may have become a learned behaviour, but the reason why the seals have started to exhibit it are not known.

Inquiry into historic child sex abuse

24/10/14.

Fiona Woolf, who has been appointed to chair the government inquiry into historic child abuse, was subjected to an interrogation on Tuesday. I strongly recommend watching the proceedings. They shed light on our weird current public culture.

Mrs Woolf appeared before the Home Affairs Select Committee of the House of Commons. She had a hard time. The essential charge against her was that she was a member of the "Establishment" and therefore (as if by iron logic) unsuitable for the task.

The committee thought she had a record as long as your arm. She is a former president of the Law Society. She is the current Lord Mayor of London. It was even held against her that she had recently led a Corporation of London delegation to Bahrain shortly after *Amnesty International* had published reports of child abuse in that country. (If such a visit was disgraceful, no delegations would ever come to Britain, since reports about child abuse here are published virtually every week).

Then there was what a left-wing lawyer on the BBC called "the evidence of dinner parties." As Mrs Woolf explained, she had, on five occasions, given or received dinner parties to or from her London neighbours, Lord and Lady Brittan. She felt it necessary to mention this because Lord Brittan, who was Home Secretary from 1983-5, is accused by some of having failed to deal adequately with allegations about child abuse by the late Geoffrey Dickens MP (though no one knows what these allegations were).

On the fragile basis of these accusations, the present Home Secretary, Theresa May, chose to erect the whole enormous superstructure of this inquiry. Its remit is child abuse in all "state and non-state institutions" from 1970 to today, how it was reported and dealt with, and where those institutions failed.

Ah, the evidence of dinner parties. It was useless for Mrs Woolf, who knocked over a glass of water in her anxiety, to protest "I am not a member of the Establishment." Her explanation for the dinners, that "I was a newly elected alderman and I needed to build my City network" (Lady Brittan was a City of London magistrate) did not help either. Nor did her elaboration that she has "held hundreds of them [dinners] since." Nor did her desire to "lay to rest any fears that I had a close association with Lord Brittan", as if the poor man were the moral equivalent of an ebola victim. In the eyes of the select committee, she was guilty.

How to remain cheerful with all around

The Spectator, 18/10/14.

Here's how to remain cheerful in the face of such a multitude of scares. I don't think I can remember a time when there have been so many scares about. They come at us from every direction, and even sometimes from out of the blue, with names we've never heard before.

Take Isis, for example, or maybe Isil (there's not even now a consensus on what to call it). Yet neither name was known to any normal, newspaper-reading person until it was already in control of half the Middle East and beheading western hostages at will. Now the Prime Minister says that we must bomb the Islamic State in Iraq because it threatens our security at home. How can such a powerful and terrifying organisation appear on the scene so suddenly and without warning?

Ebola is not such a novelty — the virus was first identified in 1976 — but the idea that we are all threatened by it is new enough. In the 37 years between that of its discovery and 2013, the World Health Organisation reported 1,716 cases of Ebola, all of them in Africa. As of this month, there have not only been 8,376 cases in west Africa alone, more than 4,000 of them resulting in death, but the odd case also popping up in Spain and the United States. The disease is now bound to arrive in Britain as well, we are assured. There will be health checks at airports on passengers arriving from west Africa, and operators on the NHS 111 helpline are being asked to screen callers for possible symptoms of the disease.

Is all this Ebola anxiety justified? It would be nice to think not, but even the usually sceptical science writer Matt Ridley, who said in his column in *The Times* this week that he doesn't often find himself agreeing with apocalyptic warnings (which is certainly true over climate change, which he either believes isn't happening, or that it doesn't matter if it is — I forget which), but that the west African Ebola epidemic 'deserves hyperbole right now. If we don't win the battle against Ebola in west Africa', he wrote, 'then we are not facing paper tigers such as Sars or bird flu, but something much more like the great plague of Justinian in AD 541, or the Black Death eight centuries later'.

Beliefs: atheism must be reflected too

Ian Burrell, Media Editor, The Independent.

letters@independent.co.uk, 27/12/14

Dear Mr Burrell,

I was interested in your article, page 2 of today's (27th Dec) *Independent* – "…more beliefs must be reflected." Yes; so why is atheism never reflected by anybody?

Atheism is a creed exactly as powerful as any religion on the planet. I have been one for sixty years, requesting at both my prep and public school that I be excused any form of 'worship' in return for which I would do any useful job, or help staff in any job asked of me. The former simply said 'no', the latter head master told me that although he respected my view the founders four hundred years earlier had laid down a decree that 'all pupils must attend worship every single day and the school governors must uphold this hereafter'. He (the HM) also said that should I take a book (Evelyn Waugh for example) into chapel and read it instead of prayers that would be breaking no rules. No objections and even eliciting a wry smile from the school chaplain – having no wish to be downright rude I did stand and kneel as appropriate.

Every single baby world-wide is born arelgious and apolitical and if, and only if, their parents are of any serious religious or political persuasion the likelihood is that the child will quite simply be brainwashed.

Finally let me point out that atheism has a track record with regard to war that borders on immaculate. Stalin was atheist but that was purely tangential to his politics.

Succinctly, atheism – in its own right – has never incited war.

Dr Richard Wood.

Play: "Piano man" washed up on Kent coast

The Guardian, 24/19/14.

The story is to be told by a London theatre company, 10 years on.

A Play by *AllthePigs* considers theories about a man who was washed up on the Kent coast and would play the piano but not speak.

The 'piano man', named as Andreas Grassl, was one of the more curious, and most haunting, true-life stories of the last decade. Dripping wet, traumatised and silent, a young man washed up on the British coast apparently unable to communicate except via the keys of a piano. The case prompted a global search and a storm of media interest before the 'piano man', as he was nicknamed, faded back into obscurity.

Ten years on, the spotlight will be back on this mysterious stranger after a London theatre company decided to put on a play based on the saga. The piece, called *The Piano Man*, will retell the story, reconsider the theories that abounded at the time – and give the tale a grand, romantic ending.

Director Sam Carrack said the story had lived with him since he read about it in *The Guardian* and *Times* back in his student days.

"I followed it closely at the time. It was such a magical story, one of those that you can't get out your mind. And then it all just disappeared. I've always wanted to know what happened next."

The director and cast have spoken to psychologists, mental health nurses and police to try to find out more about what the man may have gone through but has decided not to try to track down 'the piano' man himself.

Daniel Hallissey has the tricky job of playing the elusive character, and has learned to play the piano from scratch for the role. He said; "For me the story is a lot about the loneliness we all experience in the modern world and our struggle for identity. Finding out who we are is so difficult in these times."

The man appeared on a coastal road on the Isle of Sheppey in Kent in May 2005, smartly dressed but soaking. He was unable or unwilling to speak and ended up in hospital. There he was given a piece of paper and pencil and sketched a grand piano. The man was taken to a piano in the hospital chapel, and sat down and played.

According to some reports of the time he played so beautifully staff believed he must have been a professional musician, performing sections from Tchaikovsky's *Swan Lake* and what appeared to be some of his own compositions.

The story was picked up around the world and international television crews arrived on a bemused Isle of Sheppey to retrace the man's soggy footsteps. Police and missing people charities launched a global search for his identity.

In August 2005 the 'piano' man suddenly spoke and revealed that he was a German citizen called Andreas Grassl. He returned to his family's farm in Bavaria, with a press pack in hot pursuit. Grassl was still not speaking, at least to the media. It was left to his lawyer to explain it was actually a simple and sad story – the 20-year-old had suffered a mental breakdown while doing casual work in France and had caught a ferry to the UK and a train to Kent. But he could not remember how he came to be soaking on Sheppey. And, though he learned to play a small keyboard, he was no brilliant musician.

The play, by the *AllthePigs* theatre company, will run at the New Diorama Theatre in central London next month before touring nationally. It tells the story but also look at the rumours, claims and counter-claims that swirled around it.

Carrack said he was fascinated by the wild suggestions about who the 'piano man' was. "I loved the story of the Polish mime artist who went to police and said he was a French busker and the one that had him as a drummer from a Czech rock band." Both the busker and drummer were found at the time and ruled out. Carrack was also delighted by the story of the Danish politician who came forward to wrongly suggest the 'piano man' was her husband. "All that is just extraordinary."

The production will also look at how he was dealt with by the media – and how some turned on him after he spoke. *The Mirror,* for example, ran the headline "Piano man sham" when his identity was finally revealed. *The Guardian's* headline was "Back on the farm – the 'piano man' who can't really play."

Carrack has tentatively tried to find out what happened to Grassl afterwards and believes he is now living in Switzerland and working as a teacher. But there has been no book from Grassl, and no interviews. The company thought it best to let him be and weave what is known about him into their own version of the story. It also allowed them to create their own ending, which is much more dramatic than the reality. "We thought long and hard about contacting Andreas to see if he would co-operate. We decided not to," said Carrack.

Of course, the play may lead to a fresh search for the real-life 'piano man'. Carrack said he hoped it did not lead to unwanted intrusion. "I would feel responsible if that happened. I hope his privacy is respected. And if he comes to see the play? He would be welcome. I hope he likes it."

The Piano Man, *11-15 November, New Diorama Theatre.*

The Exclamation Mark: a personal viewpoint

November, 2014.

The exclamation mark has no place in English writing – that is in literature. That's not of course to say that it is not or never used in English writing. Of course it is – more accurately, rather over-used. Frequently and perhaps most commonly, to indicate that whatever has just been said is supposed to be funny; you might as well for example, put a comma then 'joke' in brackets, so ensuring that the reader picked up on the fact that you were not serious.

This is hideous.

Whatever made you use the exclamation mark should be implicit in the text itself – you shouldn't need to point out to the reader that he or she is supposed to smile or giggle here. After all when you're talking to somebody and make some crack you don't pause and whisper "joke" to make sure they got it. Let me a give a couple of examples to illustrate of my point.

Bill Bryson is generally thought to be an extremely entertaining author. I have read three of his books and he's certainly brought me out laughing. *Notes on a Small Island* for instance – I very much doubt if he uses the exclamation mark once during the entire book. His humour is implicit throughout.

Now turning the whole thing on its head I was looking at the publicity blurb outside a restaurant in Staithes recently and there was not one but two exclamation marks after every single sentence. It was advertising the menu and the fact that there were double as well as single rooms available, along with their respective prices and each followed by a pair of exclamation marks. What, I wondered, was the entertainment value here? It's dispensing purely helpful practical information should you be looking for somewhere to eat or stay the night. Nothing the slightest bit amusing about it.

If you were to imagine humour as a chronological spectrum I would place the exclamation mark somewhere around the nineteen twenties and thirties with Laurel & Hardy trying to get a piano down stairs, or Charlie Chaplin – pure slapstick. Crude, not sexually crude. Just unsophisticated – very 'simple' to get an idea across. John Bird and John Fortune would never ever have an exclamation mark in their scripts on *The Rory Bremner Show*, which I think was half scripted half spontaneous, yet audiences were falling about. It was politically flavoured but stands up perfectly with the passage of time long after the political implications have become history.

The exclamation mark's real authentic value is to be found in day-to-day reality to warn people of potentially dangerous situations. Road traffic accidents causing delays and route changes, road works, and new or altered direction of traffic lanes. Industrial sites and chemical plants. An articulated truck carrying dangerous chemical products. Wire-fence-enclosed electrical installations often found in odd places all over the country-side.

Currently a frequent legitimate use often comes into play in text messages from mobile phones where time and space often want to be kept to a minimum and an exclamation mark indicates quickly that what might otherwise appear cold is just meant jokingly.

The ultimate semantic irony?

! ATOMIC BOMB

Can a poker hand be life-saving?

Dr Richard Wood – a true anecdote, c. 1976

Author's note: *From memory the dialogue is not verbatim. Howeverer spiritually it's as accurate as it can be.* The Feathers Hotel *was the local hostelry in the town and the Sunday poker school comprised about ten elderly ladies who spent most of two hours laughing and gossiping – the poker being little more than an excuse – until the bar opened at twelve. They were all patients of ours and on a home visit a cup of tea was offered by default.*

Nowadays? – I don't think so.

This is not a story. It's a true anecdote. I shall forget neither the event, nor the man who implemented it. Dr George Neil, my friend, senior partner and mentor during the mid nineteen-seventies. He, sometimes invisibly, sometimes not, flavoured my professional career in general practice for thirty years.

George and I shared two things, six thousand patients and a sulphuric sense of humour; our relationship needed both.

To appreciate this tale you need to have an idea of the ambient medical climate of the time; very different from today – succinctly, unrecognisable.

First, let me describe our practice. We shared a moderately sized surgery building, which actually accommodated four doctors, the other two being 'associates', not actual partners, meaning that they were independent both financially and with patients, although we covered for all when on call at night. We were of course dispensing, and even had our own private petrol pump in the small car park at the back of the surgery building. The practice was based in the small market town of Holt, about a quarter the size of

Whitby, three or four miles inland from Blakeney, famed for its salt marshes and bird wild-life. We were very much rural, covering many small outlying villages some five to ten miles radially, so home visits of which we did many, often meant a five to twenty mile round trip. Patients over the age of seventy, we visited routinely once a month, all the names hand-written in a huge ledger which George and I kept up to date, ticking off the dates we visited as we went along and entering a † when they died. Remember computers, in this context, had not been dreamt of.

General practice was conducted on a far more intimate basis than it is today and we were often on mutual first name terms with our patients. Should you have the misfortune to need a night visit, you would be assured of having your doctor, familiar with your family, and the all the nuances that you had both grown up with, not (speaking generically), a locum from Afghanistan, comfortable with neither. Remember we're not in Tescos or McDonald's, we're with your thirteen year old daughter at three o'clock in the morning and a perforated appendix. If you want to be politically correct, dream on.

Smoking was not uncommon, even when consulting; I smoked at the time and would offer a patient a cigarette if they smoked, so joining me in a Gauloise and that unmistakeable French smell would permeate the entire building. Following our surgery at the end of the morning, George and I often joined in a glass of sherry. The two local policemen if they knew (which they didn't), would not have batted an eyelid – their families were our patients and they had plenty to thank us for over the years. In any case it was not uncommon for them to join us for a beer in The Feathers Hotel across the road. Our staff comprised a receptionist, a practice nurse, who did her own visits, two secretaries and a middle-aged lady who might best be described as a 'girl-Friday', whose job in between fags, was to do whatever nobody else did. This was considerably more than it might sound, running out to the shops for example to refresh the chocolate biscuit tin.

By complete irony some things haven't changed a jot. A shining example being one of my pals today, who is asthmatic, and is currently, some forty years later, on precisely the same drug regime as the girl in this tale; long term bronchodilators (tablets and inhalers), interspersed with short reducing week courses of oral steroids plus a steroid inhaler when needed.

But back to this tale. The girl in question was an eighteen-year-old, asthmatic since childhood and she and her family were well known to us. For the purpose of this story she is Rachel and her bouts of asthma were triggered as often as not emotionally rather than through allergy, although both played their part. On most occasions normality was restored without too much trouble through routine treatment, which is asthma plain and simple. Not so on this late summer morning.

I had about finished seeing patients for the morning, having a cup of tea, and chatting, when Rachel accompanied by her mother appeared in a state of considerable distress, clearly *status asthmaticus*. This is not, especially when you happen to be in the surgery, reason for great alarm when everything you need is readily to hand. She had already used her inhalers, both the Salbutamol and the steroid, to no avail whatsoever. So? So; the next step – intravenous steroids. The need for intravenous administration of steroids, especially in this as it happened, controlled context, should have aroused little anxiety, which it didn't. I simply gave her 100 mg of prednisolone by intravenous injection expecting that to be that.

But that wasn't that. Rachel failed to show the slightest response. The time between onset and her arrival in the surgery couldn't have been much more than ten or fifteen minutes, and with the almost immediate intravenous injection you couldn't have dreamt a more favourable scenario.

From Sally, one of our secretaries; "Hospital? Shall I get an ambulance?"

"No" from George, "far too long, by the time it gets here, then to Norwich." The Norfolk and Norwich Hospital was thirty miles away. "Put her in my room – Richard, leave her with me. You do all the visits and I'll see you later."

So, then from me – "Sally, give us the notes. Probably a couple of hours and I'll be back."

So with that I left, pondering. Rachel's mother was usually more trouble than her daughter. Not a robust woman at best. Shit – I'd never seen *status asthmaticus* fatal, but it can happen – just my luck I thought, she'd been my patient. George was ex-Royal Navy, but I couldn't imagine this situation cropping up there much. We could've just put a drip up and hospitalised her. Anyway – see what George has up his sleeve. Such situations did crop up: from whichever direction you never knew. Otherwise they wouldn't have been a surprise. But then, that's the whole point of general practice. In my more fanciful self-entertaining moments, George would be at the tables, white tuxedo, bow tie, an economically-dressed Botticellian blond draped over his left shoulder and quietly outclassing James Bond the other side of the table. A Royal Flush? ten, jack, queen, king, ace – same suit. So what were the chances of that? I was in Corpusty now – ten miles inland of Holt and at Mrs Pegg's blue back door; inside – "Earl or Builders' doctor?"

"Madge, that is a stupid question; Earl please, black no sugar, and I've got a question for you. Your Sunday poker sessions at *The Feathers*, which we all know is a covert excuse for you all to get quietly sloshed when the bar opens at twelve – have any of you ladies ever come up with a royal flush, over the last... how many years is it?"

"Well I'm almost ninety now and moved here shortly after the war so it'll be around thirty years and no, none of us ladies as you so politely put it, have ever come up with a royal flush."

"Even with that ace of spades you keep tucked in your suspenders?"

With a wry smile: *"doctor."*

"Madge, at your ripe age I can tease you, and to be teased is a compliment anyway – you're pretty boring if no one ever teases you. Now I know you don't smoke but d'you mind if I have one? Gauloises, so I'm afraid your house'll smell like a Parisian brothel, but you won't mind that will you?"

Laughing – "no no of course not, you go ahead, you've got a little time, have you?"

"Yeap – Dr Neil's sent me off doing all the visits while he reckons to score on what the rest of our profession would do with a case of death-threatening asthma. If he does it'll leave me the joke of the day, that's for sure."

So nearly two hours and five visits later I returned to Holt to find Rachel, George and our staff chatting conspiratorially, drinking coffee in our "behind the scenes" section of the surgery. Nobody, in deference to Rachel's chest, smoking. 'That's unusual', I thought.

"Rachel, better than when I last saw you. What's he done? You look great. Does your mum know yet?"

"Not yet – I wanted to settle first. In a bit."

To the girls in general – "Christ, I'll never hear the end of this."

115

And so Rachel walked cheerfully home that morning from what might be described as a "near miss", though she may have put it slightly differently to herself.

Of course her asthma never left her – that would be for life, but, to my knowledge, at least while I worked at that practice, never such a scenario again. Therapeutic convention behaved thereafter.

Later, on our own: "George, did you save her life? What did you do that I didn't. What bloody magic d'you keep up that sleeve. She got the best the pharmaceutical industry can come up with from me, didn't she?"

"She did, but when the ice gets thin the pharmaceutical industry sometimes falls through. This is a colourful illustration of the industry falling through."

"Okay. So it fell through. So what kept her afloat. What was her raft?"

"Hypnosis, Richard. Hypnosis."

"Ah, hypnosis eh? Well, hypnosis has a lot of cork to answer for. I've never heard of that."

"Neither have most people. And Richard – there's no magic. Just a technique that's all. There's nothing special. I'll teach you sometime. You do cycle racing – you'll never fall off, will you? It's no different."

"Thank you, George, I'll hold you to that. But did you save her life?"

"Richard I can't answer that can I? The only way I could answer would be if she'd died. Then the answer would have been... no."

So he did have a royal flush up his sleeve. Bond would have been proud of George, even without the white tuxedo.

RHW – edited November 2015.

116

Ignored *WhatsApp* text message – divorced

Emirates 24/7.

A Saudi husband has divorced his wife after she failed to reply to a *WhatsApp* text message. The man, who got married two years ago, sent the message from his office and waited for a response from his wife. But none came. 'Thinking something must be wrong', reported *Emirates 24/7*, 'he rushed home to find her watching television'. When he asked her why she did not respond, she said she was busy chatting with friends on *WhatsApp* and wanted to reply later. 'He divorced her instantly', the report added.

'I sent her messages on *Whatsapp* and knew she had read them because of the latest update on the application, but still she didn't answer me or acknowledged my messages', he was quoted as saying by *The Gulf News*.

The husband, in his 30s said 'he was frustrated by his wife's seemingly endless interest in using her phone for chatting with friends and family', but his efforts were to no avail.

'He had not been able to see his bride's face before their marriage', *Okaz* reported. 'When he divorced her, the bride collapsed and the wedding turned into a night of tears'.

News of the jilting was met with anger on social media. Afra wrote on one social media network: 'He caused her great pain through his irresponsible attitude, and deserves to suffer. He should appreciate that beauty is in the character, not the face. Unfortunately, many young people today are interested only in looks and ignore values and morals. May God give her a better husband who will appreciate her for who and what she is'.

Abu Nass added: 'He is not man enough to assume his responsibilities – is totally and completely insensitive. Nobody forced him to marry her – he should have insisted on seeing her face before the wedding and engagement and not wait until the wedding night. May he always be a loser and deprived of getting married at all. He is not a man and he lacks basic feelings'.

Climate change report: "…could do better"

The Sunday Guardian, 31/10/14.

We look at the data that underpins the forthcoming *Intergovernmental Panel on Climate Change* (IPCC) climate science report, detailing humanity's influence on the climate, global impacts, and solutions.

"The rate of sea level rise since the mid-19th century has been larger than the mean rate during the previous two millennia", says the draft IPCC report.

On Sunday the world's top climate scientists are expected to reiterate their warning that humanity's influence on the climate is unequivocal, with wide-ranging impacts across the planet, from rising seas to melting ice.

The UN's climate science panel, the IPCC, is currently meeting in Copenhagen to thrash out the final wording of its so-called 'synthesis' report, the most comprehensive account of the state on climate science in seven years.

If that sounds familiar, it's because it is a megamix of three major reports that have already been published over the course of the last 13 months – one on the physical science of climate change, one on its impacts on ecosystems, our food supply and how we adapt, and one on the solutions, i.e. cutting emissions from our power plants, factories, cars and farms.

A draft of the synthesis report, seen by *The Guardian*, shows it will repeat the message that there's no doubt over our role in global warming; "Human influence on the climate system is clear, and recent anthropogenic emissions of greenhouse gases are the highest in history", it says.

It doesn't mince words on the repercussions; "The atmosphere and ocean have warmed, the amounts of snow and ice have diminished, and sea level has risen."

But there is cause for hope if governments take action. It will suggest, "Measures exist to achieve the substantial emissions reductions over the next few decades necessary to limit likely warming to 2°C. A rise of 2°C is the 'safe' level governments have agreed to hold temperatures to."

Two hundred and forty-nine miles

The Telegraph, 31/10/14.

With 249 miles of track connecting 270 stations on 11 different lines, the London Underground system is what keeps the blood pumping in the city's veins.

Last year the Tube carried 1.1 billion people on 11 lines (not counting the DLR) to 270 stations around the capital and, despite daily hiccups, it remains one of the quickest if not cheapest, ways to move around. Today the extension and modernisation continues to improve travel across the city with the Crossrail project, currently due for completion by 2019. We complain about the Tube, but the chaos that ensues every time there is a strike demonstrates what a crucial artery it remains.

I've only just embraced the Underground again – I got sick of being stuck in traffic and wasting money on cabs – and am newly astonished at how cheaply and quickly it takes you around London. I grew up in Australia where there was no public transport system. I know weekends are a joke with engineering works disrupting everything, but during the week, it's an extraordinarily efficient system. What is it?

Last year the London Underground system, the first subterranean railway constructed in any city in the world, celebrated its 150th anniversary. On January 10, 1863, the Metropolitan Railway opened the first section of line between Farringdon and Paddington using steam-driven trains lit by gas lamps. Over subsequent decades, the Tube network spread to all four corners of the capital and beyond into the suburbs. Its total length today is 249 miles, it extends at its furthest point 25 miles to Chesham in Buckinghamshire and its evolution continues apace.

How is it changing lives? The Underground remains one of London's strongest symbols and encapsulates much of the capital's dichotomies – modern and old, innovative and decrepit, rapid and slow. It helps drive London's economy, transporting work-power into and across the capital, allowing it to reach and maintain its position as one of the most important cities in the world.

Saudi husband sees wife's face for first time

Mail Online, 17/11/14.

A Saudi husband tells his bride he wants a divorce during their wedding after seeing her face for the first time, when the photographer asked them to pose for pictures.

The wedding was taking place in the Western Saudi town of Medinah. Neither bride nor groom had met face to face before the ceremony and when she lifted her veil to smile for photos, the groom recoiled in disgust saying, "You are not the girl I had imagined. I am sorry, but I divorce you." The couple, from the Western Saudi town of Medinah, had agreed to marry each other despite having not met face to face – a popular custom in certain Middle Eastern countries. According to local daily *Okaz,* the bride immediately collapsed in a fit of tears, as panicked wedding guests stepped in to try to resolve the dispute.

This comes as another Saudi man divorces his wife after she didn't reply to his *WhatsApp* message.

Tory MP murdered a boy at an orgy – claim

Sunday Telegraph, 16/11/14.

Scotland Yard is investigating three 'possible murders' linked to a Westminster paedophile ring that was allegedly operating in the 1970s and 1980s.

Operation Fairbank was set up two years ago by Scotland Yard to look into the claims of abuse.

A Conservative MP murdered a young boy during a depraved sex party in the 1980s, an alleged victim of the Westminster paedophile scandal has claimed. The 12-year-old boy, who was being abused by a group of men, was strangled by the politician at a luxury townhouse in front of other victims. On another occasion the victim claims, a young boy who was around ten years old, was deliberately run down and killed by a car being driven by one of his abusers.

The alleged murders are among three that are now being investigated by the Metropolitan Police as part of a major probe into claims that a powerful paedophile ring with links to Westminster was operating in Britain in the 1970s and 1980s.

Scotland Yard, which set up Operation Fairbank two years ago to look at the abuse claims, announced on Friday it had launched a fresh strand of the inquiry, entitled Operation Midland, to probe the alleged murders.

The allegations emerged after a man, who is now in his 40s, came forward claiming to have been one of around 15 boys, who were abused at the hands of a powerful pae-

121

dophile network operating some 30 years ago. He claims after being handed to the group by his father, he was regularly picked up in cars and taken to hotels and apartments, where he was physically and sexually abused by "senior military and political" figures.

Some of the abuse allegedly took place at flats in the Dolphin Square development in Pimlico, where a number of politicians have London homes. The man, who has spoken at length to Scotland Yard detectives, said he had witnessed two murders of abuse victims by members of the group. He told the *Sunday People* that he had been in the same room as a boy, when a Tory MP throttled him to death. He described the boy as being around 12 years old and having brown hair, but said he did not know his name. The murder was allegedly witnessed by another abuse victim who was in the room at the same time, saying, "I watched while that happened. I am not sure how I got out of that or whether I will ever know why I survived."

On another occasion he claims a member of the gang deliberately ran over one of the victims, in what he described as an effort to demonstrate their power.

A third boy was murdered during a depraved orgy at which another Tory MP was present, the man has told detectives.

Child abuse enquiry: continued disarray

The Guardian, 1/11/14.

The government's child sex abuse inquiry was thrown into crisis after Fiona Woolf became the second senior legal figure to quit as chair over her links to the Westminster political establishment.

Woolf's departure is a major embarrassment for the government and raises questions about the judgment of

122

the home secretary, Theresa May, just months after retired judge Lady Butler-Sloss stepped down over similar concerns.

Woolf's exit has left the inquiry without a chair and exposed concerns about the whole process overseen by the Home Office. Victims' groups who pressed for Woolf to step down are now also calling for a much tougher judge-led inquiry. Alison Millar, head of the abuse team at law firm Leigh Day, which represents victims, said her clients were pleased that Woolf had stepped down.

"Now the work begins for a proper inquiry which listens to the survivors and supports them in giving their evidence to an experienced panel," she said.

"The terms of reference must be based on the needs of survivors and must cover the scale of abuse which is slowly coming to light across the UK."

Woolf lost the support of victims' groups after it emerged that she was a friend and neighbour of the former home secretary Leon Brittan, whose role in dealing with allegations of child abuse in the 1980s is likely to come under scrutiny.

How safe is mouldy food to eat?

BBC News Service, 22/10/14.

British families throw away about seven million tonnes of food and drink every year, enough to fill Wembley Stadium to the brim. Most of it is beyond its "sell-by" date, but how much could be safely eaten? asks Michael Mosley.

I've agreed to feast on a range of foods that have gone beyond their prime, guided by mould expert, Dr Patrick Hickey.

I realise it is going to be an unusual lunch when Hickey passes me a disposable contamination suit to wear. Before tucking in he also warns me that we will not be eating any foods that have passed their "use by" date. To do so would risk serious food poisoning.

With "best before" or "sell by" things are more flexible.

Our first course was some ageing cheddar. As he cuts away the mouldy part (being careful that the knife doesn't get contaminated by mould), he assures me the rest is safe to eat. Cheddar and parmesan are dry cheeses and because mould needs moisture to thrive, it doesn't normally penetrate far below the surface.

Some cheeses, of course, are deliberately infected with fungi. *Penicillium roqueforti* gives blue cheeses such as Stilton and Roquefort their flavour.

With most soft cheeses, however, unless the fungus has been deliberately introduced, the presence of mould suggests infection not just by unwelcome fungi but also harmful bacteria, such as listeria or salmonella. If that happens throw it away.

Next, he pulls out some bread covered in small bits of white and blue mould. He assures me that it will be fine toasted, once the mouldy crusts have been cut off. "The moulds don't go deep", he says. "The time you really need to be worried about bread is when it has black bits on it." I decide to pass.

Then he digs out some long-forgotten vegetables from the back of a fridge. The courgettes and carrots are covered in a horrible slime, which Hickey tells me is caused by bacterial colonies growing on the surface. Could I boil these up for soup?

"If you did", he says, "you'd probably develop terrible stomach ache in a couple of hours, followed by stomach cramps and diarrhoea." So best thrown out.

The Sex Change Spitfire Ace

Sunday.

Dear * * *,

In view of your seizing the opportunity to borrow Conundrum the other day, (evidently for one of your friends from your your implication) I thought I should tell you (forgive me if you watched it anyway) of a very interesting programme last night *The Sex Change Spitfire Ace* – Channel 4, 8.00 pm.

If you didn't, do try to watch it on one of the 'catch-up' channels. Fascinating – one of each: a bloke to a woman, and a woman to a man. What really surprised me was that it all took place in the 50s – years before Jan Morris. The law did catch up with one of them, but nothing to do with homosexuality (decriminalised in 1967). The surgery itself was completely uncharted territory, and extraordinarily carried out by an English surgeon, cf. J M who searched the

125

world until he found a surgeon willing to do his operation(s).

See ya soon – Richard.

Spacecraft to rendezvous with comet

Internet, 17/11/14.

The *Rosetta* Spacecraft deploying its *Philae* Lander is a spacecraft on a 10-year mission to catch a comet and land a probe on it. Launched in 2004 the spacecraft arrived at its target, Comet 67P/Churyumov-Gerasimenko, on August 6th 2014 and the lander *Philae*, made contact on November 12th 2014.

Scientists at the European Space Agency said *Philae* unexpectedly bounced twice before landing on the comet when the probe's anchor-like harpoon system failed to fire. It ended up in shadow near a cliff face on the head of the 2.5-mile-wide (4 kilometre) comet, which scientists say is shaped like a giant rubber duck. The probe fell silent on November 14th, possibly forever, as its solar batteries ran out of power.

Rosetta is the first spacecraft to accompany a comet as it enters the inner solar system. After meeting up it began a two-year study of the comet's nucleus and environment, observing how a frozen comet changes as it approaches the heat of the sun. She is named for the Rosetta Stone, a block of black basalt that was inscribed with a royal decree in three languages – Egyptian hieroglyphics, Egyptian Demotic and Greek. The spacecraft's robotic lander *Philae* is named after a similarly inscribed obelisk found on an island in the Nile River. Both the stone and the obelisk were key to deciphering ancient Egyptian hieroglyphs. Scientists hope the mission will provide a key to many questions about the origins of the solar system and, perhaps life on Earth.

It is an aluminium box with two solar panels that extend out like wings. The box, which weighs about 6,600 pounds (3,000 kilograms) measures about 9 by 6.8 by 6.5 feet (2.8 by 2.1 by 2 metres). The solar panels have a total span of about 105 feet (32 metres). *Rosetta* is the first spacecraft to rely solely on solar cells to generate power. Her payload includes 11 instruments that will provide information about how the comet develops its coma and tails, and how its chemicals interact with one another, and with radiation and the solar wind. Other instruments will analyse the comet's composition and atmosphere.

Philae, the 220 pound (100 kilogram) lander, about the size of a washing machine, touched down at 1600 GMT on November 11th. It carries 10 instruments, including a drill to take samples of subsurface material.

The planned landing site, called Agilkia after an island in the Nile is located on the "head" of the comet, the smaller of the two lobes that make up Comet 67P/C-G. Mission controllers at the European Space Agency also chose a secondary landing site for *Philae;* Site J is a sunny area, but it is also rocky, potentially making it a dangerous place to land.

Side missions

Rosetta was launched on March 2nd 2004, aboard an Ariane 5 rocket. It made four slingshot flybys to boost its speed — one around Mars and three around Earth. On its journey it passed and photographed asteroids, studied other comets and provided information about the atmospheres of Venus and Mars.

Scientists at the European Space Agency put the spacecraft into hibernation mode in June 2011 for its 373-million-mile (600 million kilometre) journey. After awakening in January 2014, the spacecraft still had four more months to travel until it reaches its target just inside Jupiter's orbit.

Comet 67P/Churyumov-Gerasimenko was first observed in 1969 by Klim Churyumov and Svetlana Gerasimenko, astronomers from Kiev, Ukraine, who were working at the Alma-Ata Astrophysical Institute in the area that is now Kazakhstan. Churyumov was studying photographs of Comet 32P/Comas Solá, taken by Gerasimenko, when he thought he saw another comet-like object. After returning to Kiev, he examined the photograph more closely and determined that it was a new comet. Its name is sometimes shortened to Comet 67P and sometimes to Comet C-G, makes regular visits to the inner solar system. It orbits the sun every 6.5 years between the orbits of Earth and Jupiter. It is among several short-period comets that have orbital periods of less than 20 years and a low orbital inclination. Because Jupiter's gravity controls their orbits, they are called Jupiter Family comets.

These comets are thought to originate in the Kuiper Belt, a region of space beyond Neptune's orbit filled with icy bodies. As these bodies collide, some are knocked out of the Kuiper Belt and fall toward the sun. Jupiter, with its massive gravitational pull, grabs some of them and changes their orbit.

Solar escort

Rosetta and *Philae* will accompany Comet 67P to its perihelion in August 2015 and travel with the comet around the sun and back into deep space until the mission ends in December 2015.

The lute's social status

Richard Wood, 2015.

Most people think of the lute as an instrument whose place rests forevermore in antiquity. Well no – not quite. When I was a medical student, I shared a flat for a while, half a mile from the Royal Albert Hall, ever since something of an icon for me. And so it came as an extremely pleasant, interesting and unexpected surprise to spot not one but two lutes in the orchestra of one of the classical Promenade concerts this year. Unfortunately I can't remember what the concert was, and I wasn't in a position to make a note. But the warming result I was left with was that the instrument does not lie entirely in medieval times, but is used in contemporary (to us) renditions of appropriate classical music.

Well for a modern builder what could be more refreshing?

Furthermore the lute is usually associated with a highbrow and formal context as the majority of illustrations which include lutes being played are heavily flavoured in this direction. But be not deceived – the instrument lay just as comfortably within Hogarth's bars, brothels and the less than well-heeled drinking nooks, crannies and grubby back-streets of east London.

Let me make an anachronistic though not so-far-fetched analogy. Some years ago *The Cod & Lobster* pub in Staithes ran Sunday lunchtime folk-music sessions, which inevitably ran well beyond legal closing time. In those days our local policeman ran things more by ear than law, and in this case "ear" always meant the song *Living Next Door to Alice* (a hit at the time). The singer was a well known regular, friend to us all, and accompanied himself with his own Spanish guitar. Five hundred years ago I would have hand-

ed him, in exchange, my lute, and there would not have
been a blink in the house.

London brutal beheading

The Sun, 20/10/14.

The Sun newspaper has faced a backlash this morning over
its "deliberately inflammatory" reporting of the brutal beheading in North London on Thursday.

Palmira Silva was found dead outside a house in Edmonton yesterday after police received calls that a man was
attacking an animal with a knife. The "sweet" 82-year-old
widow was found "collapsed" at the scene. The suspect,
who remains under police guard in hospital, was Tasered
and arrested on suspicion of murder at the scene in
Nightingale Road by armed officers, some of whom were
injured in a struggle. Scotland Yard have not yet confirmed
the motive, but have emphasised that the incident did not
appear to be terror-related, following the beheading of two
American journalists by Islamic State militants in recent
weeks.

The Sun story quoted sources who described the man as
a "Muslim convert" who had "recently grown a beard."
The tabloid's article has been described as "fear-mongering" by some, with many accusing the paper of inciting
hatred against Muslims. An insider "who worked with the
suspect", told the paper the 25-year-old man "converted to
Islam around April time" and that one of his parents was
Muslim. He talked about praying and put on a robe and
prayed whenever when he was at work.

Probe lands on comet

Daily Mail, 12/11/14.

European scientists make space history by successfully landing a probe on comet 67P/Churyumov-Gerasimenko today at 3.30pm GMT, after a 10-year mission making it the first craft in history to land on a comet.

"It's a big step for human civilisation", said the European Space Agency's director general as the control room in Darmstadt, Germany, erupted with applause celebrating immediately after the announcement.

The first image by *Philae* showed *Rosetta* 50 seconds after separation as it headed towards the planet.

Scientists were worried that thruster problems would scupper the landing, as it was not working, and harpoons also failed to fire, leaving the lander attached by ice screws in its leg. The team has not released images from the surface yet.

After a daring seven-hour descent, and despite problems with its thrusters, the *Rosetta* craft's probe, *Philae*, touched down. However controllers have revealed that because harpoons supposed to tether it to the surface had not fired, the lander may have actually bounced, effectively landing twice – and leaving it attached only by screws on its legs.

The lander announced its arrival with this historic tweet for its ten year mission. "It's complicated to land on a comet, and complicated to understand what has happened during this landing", said Dr Stefan Ulamec, *Philae's* Lander Manager. "The good news is we touched down, we had a clear signal and received data. The not so good news is that the anchoring harpoons did not fire. We looked into the data and we don't fully understand what has happened. We had fluctuations in the radio link, but it always came back again. Some of the details indicate the lander may have lifted off again and was bouncing. Two hours later this stopped. We may have landed not once, but twice."

In an emotional speech, ESA's director general Jean-Jacques Dordain said; "It's a big step for human civilisation."

Scientists hope data from the probe will help reveal how the solar system was first created 4.5 billion years ago.

Bodysnatcher turned murdered daughter into a doll

Daily Mirror, 29/10/14.

A mother has spoken of her double-grief at the brutal murder of her daughter whose remains were then dug up from her grave and mummified by a "genius" Russian historian.

Anatoly Moskvin, 47, ransacked graveyards and kept dozens of corpses of young girls in his bedroom in the flat where he lived with his mother and father.

He dressed the dead children in stockings, girls' clothing and knee length boots to make them look like dolls, even applying lipstick and make-up to their faces, and putting music boxes inside their rib cages.

The highly educated bodysnatcher marked the birthday of each of his dead victims in his bedroom in Nizhny Novgorod.

A judge has decreed that schizophrenic Moskvin – too ill to face trial for his crimes – should remain in a secure psychiatric hospital for the foreseeable future.

Following his arrest, the grave-robber told the parents of his victim accusingly: "You abandoned your girls in the cold – and I brought them home and warmed them up."

For Natalia Chardymova, 42, each new macabre report about Moskvin – arrested in 2011 – is like a hammer blow because her own daughter Olga was among 29 he secretly dug up, and dressed as a doll, and kept at home.

Olga had been horrifically murdered, aged ten, the first time she was allowed to walk alone from the family flat to her granny's apartment in the next block after her parents went to work.

"I'm ten already. I can go myself," she pleaded.

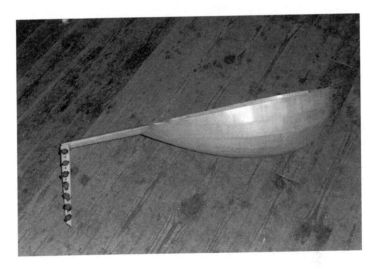

Her mother relented and she went out with her favourite green bag and blue umbrella, never to be seen alive again.

Unseen, a drug addict waiting in the lobby of her block had forced her back up to the top floor, and robbed her of her earrings, and because she tried to escape, cracked her over the head with a metal bar.

Despite searches for her body, Olga's remains with the umbrella and bag were not found for five months wedged behind pipes in the block's attic.

"We buried her on 2 October 2002.

"I could never imagine that almost exactly ten years later, on 5 October 2012, I would open her grave with the police, and find her remains had vanished.

Her coffin was empty, with a hole at the top from which he had pulled the remains.

"You can't begin to imagine it, that somebody would touch the grave of your child, the most holy place in this world for you.

"We had been visiting the grave of our child for nine years and we had no idea it was empty.

"Instead, she was in this beast's apartment."

In 7 May 2003, Natalia and husband Igor, 44, started painting a small metal fence they had erected around the grave.

The next day they came back to finish it, and felt someone had been there.

A wreath had been moved and a torment began, lasting nine years.

The same month they found a note signed with two letters – D.A. – standing for Dobry Angel or Kind Angel, how Moskwin thought of himself.

"We shivered with fear each time we went to the grave, not knowing what to expect," she said.

"These sick anonymous notes were addressed to my daughter, calling her 'Little Lady'.

"He congratulated her on all the public holidays.

"He remembered about 1 September each year (the first day of the school year in Russia) and the last school bell in May.

"He counted carefully which school grade she was about the enter, as if she was still alive.

"For example 'happy last month of your 6th year at school'.

"Imagine what it was like for us, her grieving parents, reading these notes about our murdered daughter.

"It was not at all like some sick joke but a spear through our hearts."

Sometimes the desperate parents arrived at the grave to find soft toys – stolen from other plots – and on January 1 he always put New Year decorations on the grave.

In one note, he threatened the parents: "If you don't erect a great monument which she deserves, we will dig her body out."

The couple erected a headstone in June 2003, and he penned messages on it before taking an axe to it.

Natalia reported it to the police, who were appalled but said there was little they could do.

"They told us: if you find him, do what you want to this barbarian, we won't object.

"At this point we knew nothing about Moskvin, or that by now he had already removed her, but if I'd met him at Olga's grave, I'd have killed him with my own hands."

The strain drove them apart, and they separated. Natalia wanted to move to a new flat and try and rebuild her life.

But Igor refused to leave their flat where he sat for hours on end in Olga's room.

"I just could not live in the block where my daughter was murdered.

"And Igor did not want to sell the flat, he would go into Olga's room and stare at her things. Finally I left and went to live with my mother."

Fourteen months later then got back together, and now have another child together, a son Alexei, who "has restored my faith in life."

Through all this time, the unknown visitor kept coming to the grave, leaving notes, or bending the metal holy cross.

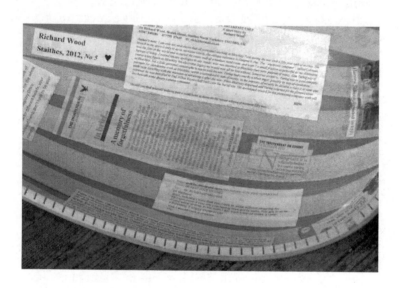

Birth of an aircraft

30/1/13.

(Moated) Salisbury Hall, 1939.
Birth of an aircraft: the banqueting hall.

Please draw to the attention of: RTeditor@radiotimes.com

Julian Fellows (re *Great Houses…*)

Dear Sir or Madam,

My wife and I have always greatly enjoyed *Great Houses* with Julian Fellows, and wonder if you might take the following into consideration.

An aircraft, just as famous as the Spitfire but for different reasons, was born on the dining table in the banqueting hall of Salisbury Hall. Some parts also in the kitchen and the prototype aircraft was built in the kitchen garden.

That seems to me irresistible for you and your associates. Julian Fellows would have a field day. To top it all, by way of contrast, there hangs on the wall of the toilet (lavatory in this context I think), in a glass case, a VIP. Not as you might first naturally think. Oh no. A Very Important Pike, caught in the moat before the first war by Winston Churchill who was often a guest.

The initial idea sprang from a quick rough sketch on the dining room table, which soon developed into working drawings. The kernel of the whole project and that which provoked heated arguments with the Air Ministry, was that it was to be built from wood, wood (by virtue of weight) was inversely proportional to speed. Thus the hand building. Of course full production, once proved, was shifted to de Havilland's factory in St Albans, but at first local craftsmen were enlisted; at that time St Albans was not the intrinsic appendage of London as now, more a town where people would know what others locally did, who did what, so when wood turners for example, were needed, local ones were enlisted. No one with such skills likes more than to be asked to produce something unusual and useful (speaking as a wood turner myself), and especially so in this case, essential for the war effort.

I hardly need say that I am referring of course to the legendary Mosquito, which aroused nothing but controversy amongst the senior air staff when it's wooden design was presented to them by Sir Wilfred Freeman whose twin engine wooden design was an outrageous novelty which they thought complete nonsense and swiftly dubbed it 'Freeman's Folly'.

They were later to change their minds.

All this is available for initial research in the book: *Mosquito: the Wooden Wonder,* by Edward Bishop, Airlife Publishing Ltd, England. ISBN 1-85310-708-5. Of course that would only be a start but I would have thought tempting. Salisbury Hall is in or near (at the time) St Albans. The Hall has been home to numerous historical celebrities dating back to the fifteenth century (Internet) and is now also a historical aircraft museum, currently closed to the public. This I'm sure, would be little more than the thinnest tissue paper to you.

I would be most grateful if you would forward this email to Julian Fellows.

Thanking you in anticipation,

Dr Richard Wood.

London Spy

email to Jack.

Recommendation: London Spy,
BBC2 9.0 pm. New series, 1/5.

Jack,

You might really enjoy this – it started on Monday, very unusual, well filmed, enigmatic and full of innuendo. Mum & I watched it on Monday night, not having any idea what it was going to be like or about. Afterwards neither of us felt like watching anything else so we switched off. I was left with not really knowing where we were, but one certainty; going somewhere and wherever that was, was going to be interesting.

Needs watching very carefully, I didn't even want to turn my head to get my tea thermos and pour. I'm sending you this straightaway in accordance with our gut reaction maxim policy, before some fucker or article waters it down coz they don't quite get it – keep in touch – hope all's going well.

all the best, dad.

Mansion tax criticised

The Telegraph, 18/11/14.

Mansion tax is "Pure and Simple"; Ed Miliband hits back at Myleene Klass.

The former *Hear'Say* singer had launched a blistering attack on the tax when she met Mr Miliband on a panel show and warned him it would hurt grannies.

In a sarcastic reference to Miss Klass's most successful pop hit with her former band *Hear'Say*, Mr Miliband said it was " 'Pure and Simple' that our NHS needs a mansion tax." The labour leader added a link to a blog which defended the controversial levy in six points.

Miss Klass left the Labour leader squirming when she confronted him on the proposed tax, telling him it will be grannies not oligarchs who suffer the worst of it.

Mr Miliband struggled to respond as the former singer and Marks and Spencer's model publicly tore into his flagship plans to charge an annual tax on peoples' homes, as the pair met on the current affairs panel show *The Agenda*.

Middle-class families were hit by Labour's mansion tax on the 20th October 2014.

Under Labour's plans, the starting rate will be £3,000 a year, and could be as much as £30,000 a year for homes worth over £3 million.

She told Mr Miliband, "For me it's so disturbing – the name in its own right, 'mansion tax'. Immediately you conjure up an image of these Barbie-esque houses, but in London, which is where 80 per cent of the people who will be paying this tax actually live, have you seen what that amount of money can get you? It's like a garage.

Miss Klass' biggest hit *Pure and Simple* topped the charts in 2001. Ed Miliband was obviously a fan.

She continued, "The people who are the super-super rich buying their houses for £140 million, this is not necessarily going to affect them because they've got their tax rebates and amazing accountants. It's going to be the little grannies who have lived in those houses for years and years."

Following the exchange Twitter users said that Miss Klass "wiped the floor" with Mr Miliband as she channelled her inner "Paxman".

Mr Miliband replied, "I totally understand that people don't like paying more in tax. The values of my government are going to be different to the values of this government."

Fellow guest Sir Christopher Meyer, former British ambassador to the US, joined in the discussion by telling Mr Miliband, "You're going to screw me royally."

Trying to diffuse the situation, host Tom Bradby said: "Ed's getting a bit isolated here."

But Miss Klass interrupted, "Ed's getting isolated because no-one thinks it is going to work. You may as well just tax me on this glass of water. You can't just point at things and tax them. You need to have a better strategy and say why is the NHS in this mess in the first place?"

Miss Klass has joined business leaders, celebrities and politicians in her condemnation of the tax. Griff Reece Jones has said that such a levy may force him to flee the UK arguing he will be faced with a "colossal tax aimed at foreigners." Melvyn Bragg, the Labour peer, has also warned Mr Miliband the mansion tax could cost the party the marginal Hampstead & Kilburn seat. In one blistering assessment of Labour's flagship tax policy, Nigel Wilson, the chief executive of Legal & General, said the party was "pandering to the politics of envy by promising to impose a levy on homes worth more than £2 million."

Others have warned the plans could drive away investment, increase unemployment and trigger an exodus of talented young people.

The real private life of the lute

Michael Praetorius in 1619 published the second volume of *Syntagma Musicum*. This was called *De Organographia*. He has long been recognised as a reliable source of data relating to musical instruments of the Renaissance period.

An important factor shadowing all instruments of this time is that they were very often vandalised, substantially modified, sometimes almost completely rebuilt.

Luthiers might surrender to the latest musical metastases, whatever that might be; a complete second neck for example was sometimes added – producing a twin necked lute. Parts were stripped to reconstruct a substantially different instrument. Lutes were often totally 're-rigged' to suit an individual player. Peg heads and whole necks were often swapped around indiscriminately.

Music of this time was slave to fashion exactly as it is today, and lutes, guitars, fiddles, violas, every musical instrument you can think of was subject to physical abuse of one sort or another and for this reason surviving instruments in their original form are unusual. At their seventeenth century height the lute's physical variance bordered on a practical example of the infinite.

One extreme, the chitarrone (1620s) – was a musical giraffe with its absurdly long neck. When the lute's popularity as the 'pop' instrument of its time (cf. the guitar in the pop music of today) gradually shrivelled, their bodies were often highjacked to build all sorts of other instruments, even a hurdy-gurdy taking an extreme example.

To conclude: if you thought the lute was the charming highbrow musical accompaniment of chamber singers sitting at King Henry VIII's feet (which probably would have bored him rigid anyway), you're not quite there.

The lute offered popular music equally to punters imbibing industrial quantities of alcohol in Hogarth's rowdy brothels. Then the walk home through the maize of narrow barely-lit east London side streets before climbing into bed with the wife, whose only weary comment would be to enquire whether Lola, the whore you'd just been servicing's bruised back was any better. "take her some more of that laudanum tomorrow night darling."

RHW

Dwarf stripper gets hen night bride pregnant

Daily Express, 9/10/14.

A dwarf stripper got a bride-to-be pregnant after her hen night celebration got a little too wild.

The woman was forced to admit that she cheated on her husband with a dwarf stripper. She had to confess to cheating on her husband with her vertically-challenged entertainer after giving birth to a child with dwarfism at a hospital in Valencia.

A Spanish news website revealed the incident today and it was quickly picked up by local and national media. Neither the hospital nor the woman have been named.

Her slip-up is said to have occurred at the start of the year. Her husband was reportedly in the dark – and of the firm belief the child was his – until it was born.

Neither her closest female friends nor her family knew she had had sex with the midget stripper but once she had her son in her arms, she broke down and confessed what had happened.

"As you can imagine no-one that sleeps with a stripper at her hen night broadcasts it, or at least they try to take their secret to the grave.

"But the protagonist of this episode had no choice but to confess and could never have pretended the boy was her husband's because of a little problem – the child was born with dwarfism."

A Spaniard who was working as a dwarf stripper expressed his surprise at the turn of events.

"I know colleagues working out of Valencia but I'm not aware of any of them getting involved in something like this" he said.

"They're mostly men in their forties and fifties and who's going to want to sleep with a man that age.

"There must be about ten of us doing this line of work in Spain.

"More often than not it's a joke thing and the women are very shy and don't even want you to touch them.

"You often go along with a normal stripper who blindfolds the woman and then you take his place and pretend it's him that's still dancing. You take the blindfold off, congratulate her and go. At most you sometimes get asked to stay behind and have your picture taken with the bride-to-be.

"I'm astonished at the idea someone's fallen pregnant like this and the woman has managed to keep it a secret even from her closest friends.

"It's certainly something that's catching peoples' interest."

Libya crisis: rival militias position themselves

The Independent, 20/5/14.

Libya is tipping toward all-out civil war as rival militias take sides for and against an attempted coup led by a renegade general that has pushed the central government towards disintegration.

In a move likely to deepen the crisis, the army chief of staff, whose regular forces are weak and ill-armed, called on Islamist-led militias to help preserve the government.

His call came after forces commanded by General Khalifa Hifter stormed the parliament building in Tripoli at the weekend, after earlier attacking Islamist militia camps in Benghazi.

The fighting has been the heaviest since the overthrow of Muammar Gadaffi in 2011, and there are signs that opposing militias and elements of the security forces in different parts of the country and with differing ideologies, may be readying to fight a civil war.

A Libyan air force base in Tobruk in the east of the country on Monday declared allegiance to General Hifter while Benghazi airport has been closed after being hit with rockets. Some 43 people were killed and 100 wounded in fighting in Benghazi at the end of last week.

General Hifter instigated the attack on the parliament building in Tripoli the capital on Sunday, was made by militiamen armed with truck-mounted anti-aircraft guns, mortars and rocket-propelled grenade launchers. The parliament leader Nouri Abu Sahmein – in sympathy with the Islamists – called on an alliance of Islamist militias known as the Libyan Central Shield to stop Hifter's forces.

Al-Qa'ida type movements such as *The Lions of Monotheism* have pledged to resist Hifter, a spokesman saying on its website that "you have entered a battle you will lose."

The most powerful competing paramilitary movements are based in Misurata on the coast east of Tripoli and Zintan in the mountains to the west. Zintan appears to be backing Hifter, whose own support inside and outside the country is shadowy with the powerful Qaqaa and Sawaiq brigades.

The latest step in the dissolution of the Libyan state underlines the degree to which the opposition has proved unable to fill the vacuum left by the fall of Gaddafi. The war which led to his defeat in 2011 was largely fought by NATO air power.

Paradoxically, both the militiamen attacking and defending the government are paid out of the central budget. In addition, Gaddafi had 100,000 men under arms who still receive a monthly salary as if they were part of the regular forces, but few turn up to work.

Al-Qa'ida type militias such as Ansar al-Sharia are strongest in Benghazi where they are held responsible for much of the mayhem. In Tripoli, Islamist militia leaders and their staffs have taken over whole floors of the best hotels such as the *Radisson Blu*.

On news of fresh fighting in Libya, the international price of oil rose to $110 a barrel for Brent crude. The Libyan oilfields had just been reopened after a prolonged closure of oil export terminals in the east of the country but are now shut again. Libyan oil output has fallen to

200,000 barrels a day, compared to 1.4 million barrels a day produced last year.

Many people in Tripoli express sympathy with Hifter's denunciations of the Islamic militias as the popular mood becomes increasingly desperate over the collapse of civil order and the central state. Hifter said "this is not a coup against the state, we are not seeking power. Terrorism and its servants want it to be a battle." The general, who in the 1980s fought for Gaddafi in Mali but defected to the United States, where he lived for many years, returned to Libya in 2011, but played only a limited role in the revolt. His hostility to the militias will go down well with many Libyans, but his forces are in practice just one more militia faction and dependent on his alliance with other militias.

Nevertheless, Libyans express growing support for anybody who can restore order and public safety by whatever means necessary.

Humour

Dr Richard Wood.

"Better never than late."

The above has to be the gold hallmark.

This piece is a very personal account, and it will be no surprise to me that some will either disagree outright, or at least find it out of line with their own experiences. But then should that not be the case there wouldn't be much point of this group anyway. I should also add that I am, not concerned here with humour's development from and during childhood, which is obviously an aspect of immense relevance – I'm sure psychoanalysts have had a field day on the subject and will have written tomes entirely devoted to this aspect. Professionally I have never had much time for psychoanalysts, and I make no apology for this. As a GP I've only referred one patient to two, * * * London.locally * * * etc independently, and they both gave up on him. The few I have encountered in a hospital context, have had their head stuck so far up their own arse they'd long lost touch with the real world. and a straightforward conversation was out of the question. When any of our friends popped in socially it was a complete embarrassment for us. He possessed neither the facility for embarrassment nor any semblance of straightforward conversation. My concern here is with the finished product. What you end up with as an adult. And what you end up with is that some people are funny, some aren't. Generalisation that might be, but I bet few would argue.

The other reason for this account's personal nature is that humour is highly person-specific. Something that tickles me might well not tickle you in the slightest. Coming at that from a different angle, I have found throughout my life that my friends have invariably shared my sense of humour, or more emphatically our sense of humour has been epoxy to our relationship, (irrespective of gender). By friends I make a cardinal distinction between real friends, and people with whom I could happily spend some time with, but who would not spring to mind in their absence – "God, so-and-so would shoot him if she heard that." Such a reaction is a mark of great respect for 'so-and-so'. In short I could never be friends with anybody who doesn't make me laugh. An odd thing is that you needn't necessarily be together at the time: your pal might for example say something quite trivial one morning, which might quite easily elicit a wry smile the following afternoon when he's half way back to London. Humour has many faces.

It is a strange thing indeed that on reflection, and very little reflection at that, although we are unique in a million ways, nearly all of them are pretty obvious in the sense that their unusualness doesn't invite deep analysis. Ninety nine percent of features of the living world, whatever example you care to pick, are species-specific. Whether it be plant or animal every 'day to day' requirement is slave (in the engineering sense) to an appropriate physiological need. The hairs on your arm rising in response to cold for example, and most obvious of course hunger shuts the door on withering away altogether, and sex ensures the continuance of your kind, whatever that might be. Some of these features have developed an association with pleasure, eating and sex being the obvious examples, but the pleasure here is a bonus enhancement, perhaps gives them a kick in the bottom to make sure they happen, as both represent, under normal ambient circumstances, our most pressing requirements.

The sore thumb that sticks out a mile is humour. Humour serves us absolutely no useful purpose whatsoever. You might argue that we, humans, have evolved to such a degree of sophistication that humour has become a necessity; the necessity to sustain our spiritual wellbeing. This does not work because there are a myriad of contexts completely devoid of humour, yet no impediment to human happiness and emotional stability. Moreover humour is often referred to as nationally specific – "oh that's such English humour." I would personally be quick to draw attention to the complete humour void that characterises the Japanese. I recall a television programme showing a family of penguins dressed up in human clothes – suits – being paraded through Tokyo streets attracting huge mirth; I can't imagine more of an insult to the penguins.

It is often said that humour sometimes provides where appropriate, a 'safety valve' for those performing some demanding, serious or dangerous job. This in my experience is drivel. It would be a silly exaggeration to say that I've heard more Irish jokes over the operating table than in the pub. It would not be a silly exaggeration to say that I've often heard considerably wittier jokes over the operating table than in the pub. The staff over the operating table know perfectly well what they're doing, and if you're funny, you're funny – operating table or pub. And they're invariably spontaneous. Television clinical soaps do the profession no favours. *Casualty* is nothing short of puerile; *Coronation Street* offering reality a marked compliment by comparison. I'm fortunate in never having been in the position of disarming IEDs in Afghanistan, but it wouldn't surprise me if the above was not equally true.

I have a life-long distaste for stand-up comedians, and paying for a seat to spend an evening watching one is way beyond me. My son Jack is a fan of Jack Dee. At least he's dry, I'll give him that, but only with reluctance. How such people perform each night on a tour Heaven alone knows. They must be as subject to mood variances as the rest of us. 'That's their job'; yes, but what a job. Perhaps taking it a bit far, but you could almost say that a comedian on an off day merits a doctor's sick certificate, as a construction worker with a broken leg. But back to their nutrition.

Humour at its best, is unexpected – a surprise. At it's very worst "did you hear the one about…?" That's not humour at all. You're in the pub for a quiet drink with your wife, joined unexpectedly by a friend, who in conversation starts on that tack, your wife excuses herself for the toilet, but when finished faces the dilemma; should she go straight back, knowing he'd be half way through repeating the punch line, just in case you'd missed it the first time, or dally a little longer adjusting her lipstick, praying he'd be finished on her return.

Humour is central to relationships, both laterally (husband and wife) and longitudinally (children). It is fair to say that, far beyond the obvious, humour not only provides a fixative to the existing cement, but also perhaps even more important, an endurative ingredient. Forgive me again for personalising, but my wife and I are constantly laughing, often I'm ashamed to admit, at somebody's expense. We have been together almost thirty five years and share an acute mutually accurate observation of people, their behaviour and reactions, and exchange information with one another by way of a glance. Words are usually redundant.

So, let me finish with the following depressing scenario, which we've probably all had before at some stage or another.

"Sarah, let's pop down the Mole for a couple (the Mole & Shovel – their local) – we've not been out for ages."

"Great, yes, that'll be nice. No, wait, George is bound to come in."

"Too early Tom, eight's more his time – we'll be well gone."

"OK, So let's go now, make sure eh?"

The Mole's an ancient grown-up pub, beams, open log fire, that sort of thing.

"Sarah, Tom, how nice, you've be AWOL for a bit, good to see you both, bit early aren't you – any goss?"

"Thought we might just miss George."

"Oh you'll be fine – much too early for him – his wife'd be at him, stuck up bitch."

"Great", and to Sarah – "Vodka?"

"Lovely, thanks."

They sat down peacefully with their drinks. But for how long? With a clatter the door opens.

Sarah to Tom "shit Tom, what's he doing this early, we're really stuck now."

"Goodness, Sarah, Tom, haven't seen you two for a bit – mind if I join you? Catch up on the goss."

"Sure, of course, please do."

George leaning over to Tom, conspiratorially "Tom, at work this morning, this bloke told me a great one about...

Sarah stood up slowly – "George please excuse me for a moment, the Ladies, you know..."

RHW

Can you really be born evil?

The Telegraph, 29/10/14.

There are many theories about why humans commit unspeakable evil, but none of them are particularly comforting. If the childhoods of serial killers are filled with abuse and hardship, then they can appear to be victims of painful circumstances. But if society isn't to blame at all – if murderers have charming upbringings and little to complain about – then could they be born evil?

Scientists in Sweden have analysed criminals who commit the most serious crimes, and believe they have identified the genes that contribute towards violence. The discovery suggests that acts of evil aren't terrifyingly inhumane, but all too human. We could all commit evil.

Brian Masters, who has written biographies of several mass murderers including Rosemary West and Dennis Nilsen, says that every human being has the capacity to commit wicked acts. The purpose of society is to curtail evil and without that influence – such as in Nazi Germany, where mass murder was encouraged – every human could commit terrible deeds.

"It's one of the most terrifying thoughts I've ever encountered and I think about it year after year," says Masters. "Whereas I am an equitable soul and would never raise my fist in anger or try to do something that is harmful to another person, I have to admit in total sanity and intellectual honesty that I could. I'm so grateful to live in a country where that is unlikely."

Masters insists that evil is an adjective, not a noun, and that when we describe someone as completely evil, we're surrendering our intellectual responsibility to analyse their actions. The early signs of murderous intent.

But although all of us could do terrible things under the right circumstances, some are more likely to do so than others. Masters says that those who are likely to commit murder usually show early symptoms in their childhood.

"The man who is addicted to murder didn't wake up before breakfast and think, 'ooh, I'm going to start murdering people'. "The frustrations in his personality were there all his life and they grow and fester", says Masters. "Whether or not you're going to do something dreadful is usually apparent before the age of five. Long before he kills somebody, he will exhibit behaviours that show he's capable of it."

Genetic links to psychopathy.

Essi Viding, professor of developmental psychopathology at University College London, says that nobody's born a killer, but that there are individual differences that affect the likelihood of developing murderous traits.

Although most children become distressed when those around them are unhappy, some are less reactive to others' emotions. "This is what psychologists call emotional contagion," says Viding. "We think it's one of the early markers of how readily you develop empathy. A lack of empathy is one of the key signs of psychopathy, and increases the likelihood of committing harmful crimes." But Viding, who focuses on the neurobiological basis of psychopathy says "parents and teachers have a strong effect on a child's mental trajectory. Growing up in a cold, mercenary environment is likely to make a child less empathetic, while a positive teacher who rewards good behaviour can help a child react appropriately to others' suffering."

"Even juvenile delinquents who have high levels of these traits can benefit from therapeutic interventions so it doesn't mean that if you have these traits that you're somehow predestined to become a psychopath," she says. "I really believe that there's no such thing as someone born evil. At the same time it would be unrealistic to say there aren't individual differences in how prone someone is to becoming evil."

A combination of nature and nurture

Simon Baron-Cohen, professor of development psychopathology at Cambridge University and author of Zero Degrees of Empathy, says that human behaviour is never more than 50 per cent determined by genetics. Although one version of a MAOA gene increases the likelihood of committing anti-social behaviour, Baron-Cohen says no gene will inevitably lead to psychopathic behaviour. "If you look at the history of people committing anti-social acts, breaking the law and hurting other people, there are strong environmental factors that predict that" says Baron-Cohen. "Growing up in an environment of criminality is one big factor, as is early neglect and abuse – those purely emotional factors."

Understanding evil.

Most people shy away from trying to understand those who commit evil, and worry that comprehension can lead to empathy for those who are guilty of terrible crime. But Masters stresses that while understanding evil is important, we should never start to pity the psychopathic murderers among us.

Quote "Someone who commits murder doesn't do so just because his parents treated him badly. A lot of peoples' parents behave badly but the children don't turn into killers. Is it because he lives in a violent society where it doesn't seem to matter so much? No, because he has a capacity to be different, he can choose to go along with the violent society or fight against it. Is it because of a psychological disorder? No, that's another excuse. But if all these things are combined – if you're badly treated as a child, if you grow up in a violent society, if you've got a psychological disorder – then you don't stand a chance. Then the murderer is himself a victim. But that doesn't mean you feel sorry for him. It means you have attempted to explain very wicked, abhorrent behaviour."

Whether men are motivated by nature or nurture, we cannot ignore the evil that exists in the world. We may flinch from understanding evil, but it's our moral duty to do so.

The Chancellor likes to keep his fridge locked

The Telegraph, 18/11/14.

George Osborne keeps a lock on his fridge in the Treasury to stop people stealing his milk, his Liberal Democrat deputy Danny Alexander has said. The fridge – which is described as double height – is also guarded round the clock by an official whose job is to prepare the Chancellor's papers, sources claimed.

Speaking to the Parliamentary Press Gallery, Mr Alexander also took a dig at Mr Osborne for being photographed with a beef burger from an upmarket takeaway. "It is fair to say that we have got our differences – I get my burgers from Burger King", Mr Alexander said. "We do share things – but not the milk – which to my amusement he still keeps under lock and key. "Yes really, the fridge in the Treasury kitchen is replete with a padlock – it must have been tough in St Paul's."

Mr Alexander also mocked Mr Osborne's "well-publicised diet and exercise regime", adding: "I don't – I just rely on running rings around Eric Pickles."

Lute and sarod

The Independent, 20/5/14.

Soumik Datta (where east meets west in music), turned down the chance to tour with Beyoncé. Her loss is London's gain, says Victoria-Anne Bull.

If you saw Soumik Datta walking down the street – complete with bouncy mane, airbrushed skin and sparkling gnashers – you could be forgiven for assuming he was a glossy Bollywood star. But Soumik (pronounced *Sho-mik)* is not an Indian cinematic performer, although he could be – his mother is an art-house film director and he was born in Bombay, the beating heart of the industry.

No, he is making a name for himself as a British sarod maestro. (The sarod is a lute-like instrument but fretless, as opposed to the more traditional sitar).

This evening Datta will be headlining at the Queen Elizabeth Hall as part of Alchemy, a celebration of artistic fusion between the UK and India. He will be performing with his musical partner and band member Austrian drummer Bernhard Schimpelsberger. Together, the duo perform Circle of Sound – an auditory amalgam of deep Indian ragas and urban beats. The pair have already toured all over the globe from Singapore, to Austria and Kuala Lumpur, but they are unleashing their new album Antihero on the audience tonight. It is an exploratory musical feast which combines Indian classical melodies with live drum and bass percussion.

"Traditionally you have to work within certain parameters within Indian classical music, it binds you to a particular style. But the rebel inside me said, 'What about all this other stuff that's in there too?'" says Datta, 30. "It feels like quite an extraordinary feat because I don't think there's been another album out there like it. This is not chilled-out lounge music. It is an anti-chill-out album with edge."

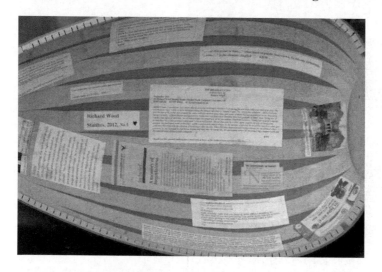

"It's hard for people to understand how an Indian classical musician has any interest in other musical genres let alone rock, drum and bass and psychedelic stuff. When they ask me what my influences are they expect me to reel off certain Indian classical names and then they're surprised when I say Pink Floyd and Radiohead. It's the sheer energy and soul they put into their live performances I admire." Datta also plays a custom-built electrically enhanced sarod he helped design himself. "It's like a baby guitar – I think it's sexy", he adds.

To put this in context, learning the sarod is apparently akin to the discipline of martial-arts training. Judging by the number of bruises down both of his arms and blood on his fingernails ("You get bleeding from the metal strings when you are strumming hard") this isn't too far from the truth. Soumik's guru in the discipline is a sarod-playing legend based in Calcutta called Pandit Buddhadev Das Gupta. In school holidays, former Harrow boy Datta, would travel to live and play with Das Gupta for three weeks at a time.

"If you learn an Indian classical instrument you should live with your teacher, so my journey was quite unorthodox", explains Datta. "It is like ninja, or some kind of martial art really, there is this real spiritual and physical discipline. The whole system of living with your guru is very important because you have to learn how to be subservient. You leave your ego outside the door and turn into a slave of the instrument."

"I still go whenever I can; he is in his eighties now. I stopped calling him teacher a while ago. I call him grandfather now."

When not with his sarod master, Datta could be found practising in the music room at Harrow. "I used to really shirk my duties in the house at boarding school and disappear into the music room quite often for eight hours. The joke was always 'Where is Soumik?' because they could never find me."

All this practice appears to have paid off. In 2006 US superstar Jay-Z contacted Datta's management and asked him to play at the Royal Albert Hall with two other local musicians. He ended up performing on stage with Beyoncé too, and was asked to join her on tour. He said no. "I was quite young at the time so I was star-struck at rehearsals, but they had this Californian vibe which meant everything was quite laid back", he says. "I don't regret not going to America. If I would have gone down that path I wouldn't have been able to explore all the other things that I have done."

Soumik Datta will be performing at the Queen Elizabeth Hall, The Royal Court Theatre, and The South Bank Centre, all in London.

Not good for dinner

London Evening Standard, 24/10/14.

Eleven members of the same family were seriously ill today after unwittingly cooking up the world's deadliest fish for their supper. The Souza family from Rio de Janeiro in Brazil, fried and served up a puffer fish they had been given by a friend who had returned from a day's sea fishing. The pufferfish contains a toxin 1,200 times more lethal than cyanide, a drop of which can kill within 24 hours. Seconds after taking their first bite all began to vomit, before losing the feeling in their face, arms and legs.

The victims, four children aged three to five, were totally paralysed before they could reach a car that would take them to hospital, according to reports.

Cristiane Souza, whose husband Jose, 41, ate the fish, said she had called her extended family living nearby for what she thought would be a delicious fish feast on Wednesday evening.

She told Brazil's RJ TV: "The fish looked so tasty so we invited the whole family. We fried it and everyone tucked in. My husband was the first to say he couldn't feel his tongue, face, or arms, then his legs went dead and he couldn't stand up any more. It was terrifying. My brother-in-law was the same. He didn't even make it out the door.

158

We had to carry them out and rush them to hospital in a car."

Grandmother Maria do Carmo said: "We had no idea it was a pufferfish. They're all in a critical condition. My grandson, daughter, and son-in-law are all in hospital. We're praying for a miracle. We put the fish on the table in the yard outside and everyone dived in. They were all saying how delicious it was. I didn't eat it because I was waiting until everyone had tried it."

The fish's liver contains the deadly neurotoxin. It is considered a rare delicacy in Japan, but chefs have to undergo two years of rigorous training and be officially licensed to prepare it.

"Strict" Catholic school – tattoos banned

Daily Mirror, 22/10/14.

Trouble: staff pulled Charlotte Tumilty aside and told her tattoos were banned in school. The trainee teacher was sent home from a strict Catholic school because of a tattoo on her neck.

Furious Tumilty, 26, had been interviewed before she was offered a role at St John Vianneys Primary School in Hartlepool, but was turned away within minutes of walking through the door. She was told that her tattoos were a problem because the school is strict Catholic, and they did not project a "professional image."

Charlotte who also has purple hair said, "they showed me to the class I was working in and a woman asked to speak to me in the office saying, "what we need to discuss is that you can still see a bit of your neck tattoo peaking out of your top."

I suggested wearing a higher-necked top but the woman said "that's not the point, it's a strictly Catholic school and tattoos are forbidden."

Royal pardon for Alan Turing

Internet: many entries.

The Queen gives a posthumous royal pardon to Alan Turing [specified date 24th December 2013], the Second World War code-breaking hero who was later convicted for being gay.

Alan Turing led the way in cracking the Enigma code at Bletchley Park, but later tragically took his own life after the 1952 conviction of chemical castration.

It is only the fourth Royal pardon since the end of the Second World War, granted under the Royal Prerogative of Mercy. This, almost 60 years after he killed himself with cyanide, gay Enigma codebreaker Alan Turing will be given the Royal pardon for the conviction which destroyed his life. Homosexual acts were only legalised in 1967.

It was requested by Justice Secretary Chris Grayling, who described Turing as a national hero who fell foul of the law because of his sexuality.

Catholic Church and Nazis in Argentina

Private email from RHW, around November 2015.

* * *

Thanks 4 your email, taken on board; can't help the following –

I had a patient when we were in Sussex – I did a 6 month locum for a GP in Ticehurst (small village, size of Staithes) and surrounding area, and one of my patients was a director of a business which had a branch in Argentina. At the end of the war the country was strategically vital, along with other South American countries, for providing a perfect escape haven for the legion of Nazi war criminals because there was no extradition treaty between South America and Europe. This bloke's office was in the capital, Buenos Aires, and as soon as I knew this I'd tell my secretary always to book him (obviously he'd some on-going quite straight-forward condition) in for my last appointment – say 6.30 isn – so we could chat. Well – fascinating plus plus. He told me of all these bars and clubs that he and his colleagues would frequent (he visited Argentina once a month) which were dominated by fading ex-Nazis, all getting completely rat-arssed and singing violent Nazi songs deep into the night. They were all in their seventies or eighties by then, 1976/7. Mum and I moved up here in January 1978. He didn't befriend any of them of course, but he told me that they collectively heavily flavoured 'the club scene'. Add to this the Catholic Church which sponsored much of it, not to mention The Pope himself: The Vatican. The Pope, Argentina and the withering Nazi National Socialism were enwrapped in some of the worst crimes against humanity ever committed, and a considerable amount of the funding (in the war's final days) was provided by The Catholic Church. Isis is currently trying to catch up. All this stuff has been common knowledge for years – I remember chatting about it with my history teacher at Yardley Court (prep school) when I was Levi's age, in other words nearly sixty years ago. One or two didn't make it to South America, choosing other escape routes – Spain for instance. I well recall Adolph Eichmann who was caught and stood trial in this country for war crimes. I remember lying on my tummy in my room at Harrow following the story in *The Telegraph;* he was hanged.

Front page news. The Catholic Church's not-so-distant history and less palpable links do surface from time to time, and The Pope's liaisons with under-age choirboys hardly helps, but somehow it retains a flimsy shred of credibility – beats me how.

Anyway I obviously won't say owt/ought/ anything to Augustina (promise). Lovely name – wot d'you call her? Aug, Augy, Orgie… (hard 'g' of course)…

I'll see ya @ The Ritzy 4.30 ish don't worry about time. Quite happy chilling – just have a drink etc, but won't eat out coz we'll do that later. Look forward 2 ceeing u.

The properties of *Lignum vitae*

29th September, around 9pm.

Dear Albert,

Just read your email – that's interesting about the "piece of wood amongst your clutter" – 2 things come to mind. The wood that's self-lubricating, and famous for it, is *Lignum vitae*. It was for this reason used for the bearings of the prop shafts in early steam ships – its 'oiliness' was perfect. It's the heaviest wood on the planet, with a specific gravity of 1.2.

It's not particularly exotic and to be found world-wide in a wide variety of industrial settings. It's quite easy to get on the appropriate 'wood market' Exotic Hardwoods for example. Quite easy to work and is green. It's not African – Columbian and along with cocaine (its next door geographical neighbour) props up the Columbian economy. Saltburn pier is much more likely to be jarrah, but greenheart is just possible, but for a small town the size and importance of Saltburn, I doubt g/heart would merit the extra expense. I'll post you (Castleton add YO21 2EL) a sugar cube of g/heart and jarrah. Pop 'em in a glass of fresh water – the g/heart sinks like a stone, jarrah will float (sp gr 0.8, as opposed to 1.2). Don't forget the pub lunch (on me) in Staithes, and a quick glance at my workshop.

The best Richard
– keep an I out for the little parcel…

Conclusion – the wood is greenheart.

Prof Stephen Hawking: England's chances

The Independent, 29/5/14.

He said; "If only I had whispered this in Chris Waddle's ear before he sent the ball into orbit in 1990; Use the side foot rather than laces and you are 10 per cent more likely to score."

"A 50°C rise in temperature reduces our chances of winning by 59 per cent. We are twice as likely to win when playing below 500 metres above sea level."

"The statistics confirm the obvious. Place the ball in the top left or right hand corner for the best chance of success – 84 per cent of penalties in those areas score."

"The ability of strikers to place the ball results in them being more likely to score than midfielders and defenders."

"There is no evidence that it's advantageous to be left or right-footed but bald players and fair-haired players are more likely to score. The reason for this is unclear. This will remain one of science's great mysteries."

Paddy Power, spokesman for *Paddy Power,* said "the modern game is so full of statistical analysis that for us it was a no-brainer to call on Professor Hawking to give England some help."

Famous *Paul the Octopus:* the tentacled creature gained legendary status correctly predicting the outcome of eight matches at the 2010 World Cup, including Germany's thrashing of England and Spain's victory over the Netherlands in the final. He cost bookmakers thousands after floating languidly towards boxes of mussels draped in the colours of competing teams in the tournament.

He died in his sleep in October that year, but his former carers at the *Sea Life Centre* in Oberhausen, Germany, decided he should be given a shrine to mark his seemingly expert predictions.

A Brief History of Stephen Hawking: how the disabled genius rose in adversity to become one of the world's great academics.

Professor Stephen Hawking, 72, has lived with debilitating motor neurone disease since the age of 22, but despite this cruel struggle he still became the world's most renowned astrophysicist.

He is a sufferer of the most common form of motor neurone disease – amyotrophic lateral sclerosis – which has robbed him of almost all physical movement.

He is an exceptional case, having survived for more than 40 years, despite doctors giving him just two years to live when first diagnosed.

In his incredible life his countless scientific papers, best-selling books and numerous awards have earned him comparisons with Albert Einstein and Sir Isaac Newton.

But he is as much a celebrity as he is a scientist, appearing on the TV cartoon *The Simpsons,* starring in *Star Trek* and providing narration for a British Telecom commercial that was later sampled on a Pink Floyd album.

In the 1970s, already confined to a wheelchair, he produced a stream of first class research, including probably his most important contribution to cosmology. This was the discovery of *Hawking radiation,* which allows a black hole to leak energy and gradually fade away to nothing.

By applying quantum mechanics to black holes, he had taken the first steps to combining quantum theory with general relativity. One describes the universe at the sub-atomic level, and the other at very large scales. Bringing the two theories together is one of the great unfulfilled goals of modern physics.

In the 1980s Professor Hawking and Professor Jim Hartle, from the University of California at Santa Barbara, proposed a model of the universe which had no boundaries in space or time. The concept was described in *A Brief History Of Time*, which sold 25 million copies worldwide.

In recent years Professor Hawking has examined the relationship between science and religion, writing a 2010 book, *Grand Design*, which argues that evoking God is not necessary to explain the origins of the universe. He met the Pope at a scientific event hosted by the Pontifical Academy of Sciences in 2008.

A computer hacker walks free

The Sun, Wednesday 15 October 2014.

Computer hacker Hector Xavier Monsegur, better known by his screen name 'Sabu,' walks out of Manhattan's Federal Court after his sentencing in New York. The FBI is facing questions over its role in a 2011 hacking attack on Rupert Murdoch's *Sun* newspaper in the UK after the publication of chat logs showed that a man acting as an agency informant played a substantial role in the operation.

In July 2011, a group of hackers known as *Lulzsec* – an offshoot of *Anonymous* – posted a fake story about the death of Murdoch, penetrated several *News International* (now *News UK)* corporate sites, and claimed to have obtained gigabytes of material from the company's servers. *The Sun* website after it was targeted by computer hackers, visitors to the website were redirected to a hoax story about Rupert Murdoch's suicide. The attack was so successful that the publisher took down the websites of *The Sun* and *The Times* while technicians worked out the scale of the hack.

Unsealed documents obtained by *Motherboard*, the technology channel operated by *Vice*, and seen by the *Guardian*, show Hector Xavier Monsegur – known widely online as

166

"Sabu" and frequently referred to as the leader of *Lulzsec* –
played an active role in the operation.

The chat records show Monsegur encouraging others to
break further into *News International* systems, claiming to
have sources at *The Sun*, and even apparently helping to
break staff's passwords and to source files for stealing.

Monsegur was, however, at that time operating under
the direction of the FBI, who had arrested him weeks earlier and cut a deal that kept him free if he helped to track
down and secure the convictions of others in the group.

The close involvement of an FBI asset working under
extraordinarily close supervision in a hacking attack on a
media outlet ultimately owned by a US-listed company is
set to raise further questions about the agency's approach
to tackling online crime.

Monsegur, who faced a maximum of 124 years in
prison, was released earlier this year in exchange for his
"extraordinary" cooperation with the FBI and is currently
on a 12-month supervised release programme. He is believed to have cooperated with authorities because of his
role as sole carer for two young relatives. He has had no
contact with the media since his release.

The chat logs, which are more than 380 pages long,
show the *Lulzsec* group working together over several days
to hack into *The Sun*, talking in the relaxed (and often mis-
spelled) manner of online conversations.

The chat, in a private channel aptly named "#sunny-
days", jumped between talking through reasons to attack
the newspaper, what to do when in, and technical advice
on how to operate the hacks.

Some members of the group had already secured limited access to servers owned by *The Sun*. Sabu immediately
encouraged them to go further, and obtain email records.

At the time, others in the channel were focusing on merely embarrassing *The Sun* by running a false news story – which they did – or replacing home pages with pictures of internet memes, such as *Nyan cat*.

Later, another hacker obtained encrypted login details of multiple *News International* staff, but was unable to de-crypt them and thus obtain the usernames and passwords. Sabu offered to assist at this point, and later provided the password details. At various stages in the course of the conversation he also claimed to have obtained mail records from HSBC bank, and details on the Qatari royal family.

Visulate: birth of a word

Richard Wood.

The English language is famous for the volume of its vo-cabulary. I'm told that the Oxford English Dictionary holds roughly twice as many words as its French equiva-lent. So we can, or have the facility to, express ourselves with an unprecedented degree of precision, providing, of course, that we have at our fingertips sufficient under-standing of this terrifying armoury of words. Look, for example, at the words presume and assume. Leave out the meaning itself, and consider the reason why they differ. They don't of course always differ. Sometimes they can be interchangeable, sometimes not. The reason being that each word carries different built-in implication. Sometimes it coincides, sometimes it doesn't.

If you don't believe me try Fowler's *Modern English Us-age*, p74, and if you can follow that good luck to you. I'm certainly not going to reproduce it here.

All languages contain the built-in facility of articulacy, for the requirements of their users, whatever they might be. Whales, hedgehogs and humans, articulate in different ways. Swahili and Chinese choose the widely used technique of investing a variety of meanings into the same word by altering its spoken inflection. In the same way, for instance, that you might spotlight a wooden cube from different angles. Its appearance changes infinitely, but it's the same cube. So Swahili multiplies its originally small vocabulary with the spotlight. We, the English, start with a large number of different sized cubes, and light them from the same direction.

The point of all this is simply that you should be used to this comprehensive lexicon, which for years has been to you like a four- wheel drive BMW truck, capable of anything, it comes as a special surprise when confronted by a track so steep and snowy, that you can't quite get there. So? A new way. A new word.

For example, I am a photographer. More than that, I am comfortable with the work of say, Edward Weston, Minor White, Bob Cappa, Elliot Erwitt and Cartier-Bresson – which means? Which means I can read the image.

Here our language collapses; here is no existing word, which describes what others have termed the visually literate. But what clumsy nonsense. The two words are incompatible by definition.

So let's coin the word *VISULATE*, which can legitimately be equated with literate and numerate.

Should the *Oxford English Dictionary* approach me, and say: " Richard – this *visulate* – what does it actually mean?" I would answer by exploring the word from three perspectives, outgoing, incoming and reciprocal. The word describes the human facility for understanding, interpreting and inferring the implied information from a visual image; the ability to absorb what the author (the portrait painter or the war photographer to give a literal analogy) has intended to convey. And so, of course, it equally describes the generator of the information – the artist, in this case the photographer. Both, you assume visulacy from. That takes care of incoming and outgoing. But its converse, its reciprocal, that's another question.

Somebody expressing themselves in a visual language, whether it is painting, photography or etching, requires a reciprocal intellect to read his or her work, not with the precision associated with words or numbers, but in more blurred, yet perceptive way. I thought ivisulate, would be in keeping with innumerate and illiterate, but my sister, who has the irritating habit of sometimes but not always being right, says no; it should be invisulate. The negative, if it's before a v... should be in rather than i..., as in invisible. She is a professional portrait artist, and is certainly visulate but not always right.

Always enjoying getting one over on me, she, behind my back, was heard to say – "to say ivisulate you'd have to be illiterate."

When, in the distant future, you browse through the Oxford English Dictionary trying to find a way of describing those who can't appreciate that Heaven's Gate was Michael Cimino's masterpiece to those who claim not to be able to understand it – there it will be, all ready for you; ivisulate.

So, where does that leave us? It leaves us with images by Tony Murphy and Jackson Wood and one word by Richard Wood, each of which demand careful consideration. Should you place these in order, the image has to precede the word; the facility for reading the image required the word. Murphy's images demand a sophisticated and visulate audience, an audience that demands, indeed expects, visual eloquence. His photographs demand a reciprocal sensitivity, which reaches perhaps a few, but nevertheless, the few who are visulate.

Visulate *a, phonetic vizuⱻt [Wood/ Murphy]* – *1. Visually edu-cated, articulate, cf. literate, numerate. 2. Able to express oneself vi-sually with a precision usually associated with words or figures. 3. Able to read and/ or interpret imagery 4.* Visulate *v. (long 'a') To facilitate the discussion and/ or interpretation of imagery. 5.* Visula-tion *n. the facility to read an image. 6.* Ivisulate *antonym, the in-ability to read, understand or interpret an image.*

Richard Wood.
Revised 2010.

Mapp and Lucia

dr_dick@hotmail.co.uk

feedback@radiotimes.com, 29/12/14.

Mapp and Lucia is a masterpiece. The entire team who put this piece of drama together; writer, director, producer, photographer and all the actors had a total grasp and un-derstanding of something very unusual – sailing close to the wind. They sailed as close as you possibly could with-out stalling. I can't remember any television getting remote-ly near what they achieved. Every single frame, every line of dialogue was clever, witty and often very funny. But to get all this you had to pay attention.

Congratulations to the whole team. My advice to all viewers out there who have any interest in grown-up, so-phisticated television watch *Mapp and Lucia.*

Dr Richard Wood.

Rising Damp

feedback@radiotimes.com, 19/3/15

Dear Sir or Madam,

It is commonly thought that drama, sit-coms, films, television series 'date' as time passes. Clothes and hair fashion both male and female, being probably the most obvious examples. However the most interesting feature of all by a long chalk, is humour. Humour is the most elusive and complex facet of our human-ness imaginable, and if you doubt that try describing it to someone else in your own mind – you won't get far. For a start it serves no useful physiological purpose whatsoever. And that's unique within the living world.

So where does that leave *Rising Damp?* the recently resurfaced television series from 1978. It leaves Leonard Rossiter turning that notion upside-down, holding it by the ankles and gently tapping its head on the floor. Its wit and performance are light-years in front of the majority of currently broadcast sir-coms. Before you go anywhere it torpedoes that frightful fashionable toxic vogue "political correctness." That gives it five stars before you've even started.

So let me thank and congratulate ITV3 and all *Rising Damp's* crew for doing exactly that.

Yours etc,
Dr Richard Wood, North Yorkshire.

How to stop motorist driving the wrong way

Mail Online, 31/10/14

Luke Goodall, 26, was seen driving the wrong way down the A1(M), near Stevenage, for eight miles before colliding with a police car.

Sergeant Karl McDermott forced Goodall to stop by driving in his way, positioning his police car in the way of Goodall's Ford Fiesta to bring it to a halt.

Goodall was seen driving the Fiesta south along the northbound carriageway at junction 7 of the motorway at 1.40am on August 7th. He narrowly avoided crashing into several vehicles heading in the opposite direction before police arrived. Sergeant McDermott was about to set up a rolling roadblock when Goodall arrived, slowing down before the collision, bringing the Fiesta to a stop.

Video footage shows Sgt McDermott driving the correct way along the motorway when a pair of headlights appear on the horizon – on the wrong side of the central reservation. He slows down, quickly positioning himself in front of Goodall's vehicle before carefully shunting the car, bringing it to a halt. With Goodall seemingly unaware of what has happened, McDermott runs from the police car and drags Goodall out of the Fiesta.

Meanwhile other officers put up a road block on the carriageway to reduce further risk of a collision and Goodall was arrested for dangerous driving as well suspicion of drink driving.

He was today jailed for eight months for dangerous driving and failing to provide a specimen. He was also disqualified from driving for three years and will have to take an extended driving test before being able to get behind the wheel again.

Sgt McDermott said; "Despite the time of night there was still fast-moving traffic on the motorway and the darkness meant drivers had minimal time to avoid the oncoming vehicle. I would like to take this opportunity to thank the many witnesses who came forward to provide evidence in this case. It is clear that a number of drivers were left in genuine fear for their lives after describing how Goodall only missed them by inches.

Goodall is extremely lucky that he did not cause a serious collision that could have resulted in people getting killed or seriously injured. At the time he had no regard for how much danger he was in."

Sentencing Goodall at St Albans Crown Court, Judge Michael Baker commended Sgt McDermott for his 'significant and brave actions in bringing [Goodall] to a stop'.

Inspector Phil Bloor said; "In some circumstances and always as a last resort when there is an immediate risk to life – as was the case in this incident – the only way to stop a dangerous driver is to put a physical barrier in their way. In this case I am certain that the actions of Sgt McDermott and other road policing officers on that night were all that stopped a serious collision from happening. The driver was removed from his car for his own safety. Given where the cars were stopped – the fast lane of a motorway – it was imperative that officers acted quickly to arrest him and remove the danger to the public, to themselves and to Goodall himself. I hope this video footage brings home some of the dangers present on our roads and the lengths police officers will go to keep them safe for everybody."

Pope rents out Sistine Chapel to Porsche

Sunday Guardian, 24/10/14.

Porsche will hold a concert followed by a "gala dinner" in the Vatican museum, "surrounded by masterpieces from world-famous artists."

The Sistine Chapel is the most famous — and instantly recognisable — symbol of the Roman Catholic Church. It is here, under the magnificent frescos of Michelangelo, that Popes have been elected for centuries. It is here too that reigning Popes kneel in private prayer. Now, in an unprecedented commercial deal, Pope Francis is renting out the 15th century chapel to Porsche for a private event of another kind; a concert, followed by a "gala dinner" in the

Vatican museum, "surrounded by masterpieces from world-famous artists such as Michelangelo and Raphael."

It is the first time in its ancient history that anyone has been allowed to hire the chapel, the proceeds of which will go to charities for the poor and homeless. The Vatican has refused to disclose how much it will earn from its deal with the Porsche Travel Club but with a spokesman for the German corporation calling the event "a once-in-a-lifetime opportunity", it is expected that the fee will be very substantial. Curiously, just prior to the announcement, the Vatican had stated it would cap the number of tourists allowed inside the chapel to the current total of six million to protect the frescoes from pollution. Some Vatican observers have expressed fears at the deal, not least because barely two weeks ago, the singer, Justin Bieber, was discovered kicking a ball around the Vatican during a £16,000 private tour.

Hurricane Gonzalo and Network Rail

Daily Telegraph, 20/10/14.

Dozens of Network Rail teams are dotted around the country in anticipation of 55mph winds which threaten to bring down branches and trees over tracks during the morning rush hour. With many trees still in leaf, the strong westerly winds – set to reach up to 70mph in coastal areas and 80mph in northern Scotland – are also expected to dump large amounts of foliage across the railway network. So-called 'leaf-busting' engines will be deployed on Monday night to clear foliage from tracks as winds pick up to reduce the likelihood of morning services being affected by leaves on the line.

Network Rail said it was not prescribing any changes to services ahead of the storm, but added that severe conditions could require drivers to take extra care when accelerating and braking which could have a knock-on effect on timetables.

Hurricane Gonzalo: 75 mph winds to hit UK

The Guardian, 20/10/14.

Remnants of Hurricane Gonzalo are set to arrive in Britain later on Monday bringing strong winds and heavy rain. Gusts of up to 75mph in coastal areas and 65mph inland will tear across much of the country bringing disruption to many areas, particularly to travel.

The area of rainy, windy weather will then move eastwards, varying in intensity across the UK, with the strongest gusts on the coasts. We can expect gusts up to 65mph in the north west tomorrow morning, and up to 50mph in central and eastern parts of England in the afternoon. It will remain windy tomorrow evening, but winds will gradually die down as the weather system passes.

The Met Office has issued a yellow, 'be aware', weather warning.

A spokesman said: "The strongest winds are expected on Tuesday as the low pressure clears eastwards. There remains the potential for localised disruption to travel, especially as the strongest winds will coincide with rush hour in places. Fallen leaves impeding drainage increases the risk of surface water affecting roads, while some damage to trees is possible, given that many are still in full leaf."

Hurricane Gonzalo last week caused widespread damage and a power blackout when it hit Bermuda. The Bermuda weather service had warned residents not to go outside when the storm's calm eye moved in, but some ventured out anyway to do quick damage assessments, noting that porches were destroyed and power lines were downed.

Royal Navy frigate *HMS Argyll* has arrived at the tiny British territory to assist in the relief effort if required. The vessel is equipped with a helicopter and a number of small boats to help with reconnaissance and transport, and is also able to assist with power generation, communication and water supplies. Defence Secretary Michael Fallon said; "Royal Navy personnel are trained to respond to situations such as this and *HMS Argyll* is well resourced and ready to provide assistance to the people of Bermuda."

18,000+ requests to remove Google links

Daily Mail, 12/10/14.

Britons have made more than 18,000 requests to remove Google search links under the "right to be forgotten" ruling.

The company introduced its request process following a European Court of Justice ruling in May, that links to irrelevant and outdated data should be erased on request from searches within the EU.

The move sparked concerns over censorship of material which is accurate and in the public domain. Google listed some examples of the types of requests that are made from the UK including; "A media professional requested that we remove four links to articles reporting on embarrassing content he posted on the internet. We did not remove the pages from search results."

Another involved a public official who "asked us to remove a link to a student organisation's petition demanding his removal. We did not remove the page from search results."

"A doctor petitioned the search engine to have more than 50 links to news stories about a botched procedure removed, and while three that did not mention the procedure were removed from search results for his name, the rest remained."

And in an indication of how the site must be aware of national laws it said; "A man asked that we remove a link to a news summary of a local magistrate's decisions that included the man's guilty verdict. Under the UK Rehabilitation of Offenders Act, this conviction has been spent. The pages have been removed from search results for his name."

Facebook is the site impacted most with 3,353 links removed Europe-wide, YouTube follows, leaving profileengine.com third with almost 2,400 posts removed.

The "right to be forgotten" requests can be made by more than 500 million people living in 32 countries.

A mind-reading device

California Telegraph, 31/10/14.

A mind-reading device invented by scientists of The University of California to eavesdrop on the 'inner voice' – surprise, surprise? I don't think so.

Scientists at the University of California were able to pick up several words that subjects thought using a new mind-reading device. Brain activity could be turned into speech with a new mind-reading device designed by the University of California.

It might seem the stuff of science fiction, but a mind-reading device is being developed by scientists which can eavesdrop on your inner-voice.

178

Researchers at the University of California, Berkeley, have developed a machine and computer program which converts brain activity into sounds and words.

Speech activates specific neurones as the brain works interpret the sounds as words. Each word activates a slightly different set of neurones. Now scientists have started to develop an algorithm that can pick up the activity and translate it back into words in the hope it might help people who are unable to speak.

"If you're reading text in a newspaper or book, you hear a voice in your own head", Brian Pasley told New Scientist magazine.

Professional wit – deludes many people

Letter to The Radio Times, March 2013.

It has for many years been a source of great irritation to me that the general public are led to believe that the professions in general, while performing their function whatever that might be, do so with little or no humour, wit, interactive teasing or a sprinkling of plain ordinary jokes. This impression is almost unanimous to crime, medical, drama and all the soaps wherever reference is made to a professional context.

My viewpoint is one of thirty years experience as a doctor in both hospital and general practice. It has been my pleasure and privilege to earwig far cleverer, wittier, invariably spontaneous cracks while removing a gall bladder (for example), than I have later in the pub that same night. Triggered often by just pressing a little too hard, or perhaps not cutting quite enough, neither bearing the slightest reflection upon the skill of the surgeon any more than a missed computer key by a lawyer's secretary. Both, given time, will be a statistical certainty and probably elicit the

179

same response. The operatives know perfectly well what they're doing, and quite capable of talking at the same time.

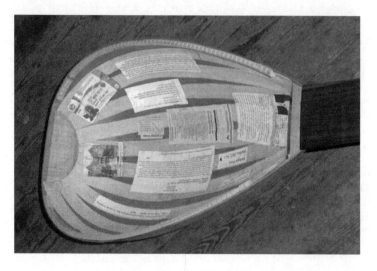

In the surgeon's case the subject of jest might well be at the expense of colleagues, hospital administration, the patient themselves even, but then when an anaesthetic holds the trump card he or she is on safe ground. Furthermore such lightening of the serious, nearly always involves swearing – aways white-washed by drama writers, yet the words fuck and shit rest as comfortably in the operating theatre as in Afghanistan's front line. Moreover it has to be said that in the medical setting their funniness might well be reinforced by female surgeons (? with deliberate intent), and I certainly once worked under a colourful woman who deliberately got the most mileage out of this. Furthermore, enhancement is even more exaggerated when the surgeon involved holds a high profile on the national stage, which in a teaching hospital almost by definition, many do. In

Kenya I always recall a rather loud, over-extrovert Scottish woman consultant during our removal of a large gastric cancer from a Masai warrior's abdomen – "fuckin 'ell – never seen one that size" – I often wondered if she could pull that off in Swahili.

So; my point is that the vast majority of screen writers seem to be deluded by the idea that seriousness of subject is inversely proportional to humour, crude or otherwise, a delusion I find sufficiently irritating to prompt this letter.

A shining exception is Sally Wainwright *et al* for the masterful series *Scott and Bailey*. Again, only my own view, but this is television at its best. The crime as the focus is often belittled by the relationships and especially dialogue, amongst not only the two protagonists, Rachel and Janet, but also their colleagues and boss. It contains just such appropriate swearing as described, resulting in a picture of complete reality. All their marriages or relationships are in tatters, and she makes the most out of this, doubling both its entertainment value as well as its tribute to everyday life.

I have notably and deliberately made no allusion to war as this is well beyond my own experience, but am quick to offer humble apologies to any such readers who might find my view untenable.

Dr Richard Wood.

Experts blast "medical tourism"

Daily Express, 24/10/14.

After the death of a British woman during a botched cosmetic procedure in Thailand, experts have spoken out against so-called "medical tourism."

Travelling abroad for cosmetic surgery can be dangerous. The woman, who has not yet been named, is understood to have died when she was given an intravenous anaesthetic as part of a procedure on her coccyx. The doctor who carried out the operation was uncertified and has now been arrested and charged in connection with her death.

The tragedy echoes the death of Londoner Claudia Aderotimi, 20, who died when liquid silicone was injected into her buttocks in a procedure designed to enhance her bottom. She arranged the surgery online and then travelled out to Philadelphia, USA and the procedure was carried out in a hotel. She experienced chest pains and difficulty breathing and preliminary post-mortem examination showed that her lung had filled with silicone, causing a fatal pulmonary embolism.

Research conducted by Confused.com in 2013 found that nearly a third of Britons who have undergone cosmetic surgery travelled abroad to do so, but many are left unhappy with the results, and in rare incidents like the above, even end up dead. Some companies even advertise 'plastic surgery holidays'.

As soon as you venture outside Europe you really are exposing yourself to significant risk. Last year a study by Leeds University into cosmetic surgery holidays revealed a shocking 16.5 per cent complication rate with nearly 1 in 10 patients needing assistance from the NHS after arriving home.

It seems this is a growing trend – a survey of members of the British Association of Aesthetic Plastic Surgeons (BAAPS) found that over 60 per cent of surgeons reported an increase of 25-35 per cent in the number of patients seeking help for problems following cosmetic surgery performed abroad.

Michael Cadier, consultant plastic surgeon and President of BAAPS said "The Health Service at one stage was getting a lot of patients coming through either dissatisfied or having problems following the surgery.

"I've been involved myself with patients who have had breast implants put in and the implant is popping out through the skin. I've had patients who've had eyelid surgery and their eyes aren't closing so there are problems with exposure of the cornea. These types of things are not common but certainly not an unusual event."

Confused.com's survey found that 25 per cent of people who travel abroad for surgery do so to save money.

Mr Cadier said: "It's perceived as being cheaper; for example if you get a breast augmentation procedure undertaken in the UK, it costs between £4,000 and £7,000 depending where in the country you have it done and by whom. In the far east you're probably talking about half that."

Life in Squares

feedback@radiotimes.com

Ref: Life in Squares, BBC2 Monday 27/7/15, 9pm.

Dear Sir or Madam,

The Bloomsbury Set was supposed to be a group of intellectual, convention-defying, forward-thinking radicals and as such you'd expect their dialogue to reflect such.

Well *Life in Squares* does no such thing. The drama is no less than a shining example of missed opportunity and pure insult to the 'set' it pretends to portray. The script is spectacularly boring and completely without any wit whatsoever. And wit was perhaps recognised as the kernel of the group. Virginia Woolf would turn in her grave.

Dr Richard Wood,
emailed 10pm 28/7/15.

Why daughters cost £5,700 more than sons

Daily Telegraph, 24/10/14.

Parents will pay £32,700 for living costs and extras after their child has reached adulthood, a survey claims.

While Harry Enfield's Kevin might resonate with many parents, apparently daughters are costlier than boys. Comedy duo Kevin and Perry may bring back memories of parents' own moody teenage boys, but once children reach adulthood it is daughters that prove the most costly.

After they reach 18, daughters apparently cost their parents £5,700 extra. Parents will fork out £32,700 for children aged 18 to 30 on average, paying for university and accommodation costs, alongside extras like a property deposit, car and wedding.

Between the age of 18 to 30, parents will pay £5,000 for their child's higher education, £5,000 for a house deposit and £5,000 for getting married, the research suggests.

It is claimed that a female child will get an extra £700 for their property deposit and £1,000 for their wedding, compared with male children, based on the responses of 1,000 parents aged over 50.

There's also a premium on supporting adult children in Britain's most expensive postcodes. Supporting an adult child in London costs £68,000 until they are 30, with biggest expenses coming from higher education (£10,500) and a property deposit (£10,300).

"Full-nest" parents, who continue to support children after they reach 18, also face higher costs in the Midlands and North East. Even before adulthood, the cost of raising a child to age 18 is estimated to be £227,266 according to research from the *Centre for Economic and Business Research*. The study also found that one in five parents are delaying having another child due to cuts in benefits and higher living costs.

Returning a forgotten book

Ref. the book: The Pianist, Wladyslaw Szpilman, 13/7/15.

Ms Katrina Beale,
20A Potter Hill,
Pickering,
YO18 8AA

Dear Richard,

Whilst looking through my bookshelf the other day I came across your book! I can only think you may have lent it to me or I idly took it with me after I had visited your surgery. I don't remember stealing it!

It is about 25 years ago that I lived in Staithes so I have kept it safe for you and I'm now returning it.

Have you missed I wonder?

With best wishes,
Katrina Beale

17th July 2015

Dear Katrina,

Well what a surprise. Thank you so much for returning the book. When the parcel arrived this morning it certainly had me thinking. I must say I have no recollection of the whole scenario whatsoever. 25 years ago certainly fits. I've been retired well over ten years. You may or may not have read the book – it's not brilliant but interesting nevertheless. A film (same name) was made of it too, but rather weak. If you're interested I can send you the DVD, but imagine this whole thing just happened by chance (the book in my surgery etc), and you have little actual interest at all.

Anyway thanks again – if you have any comments email is by far the easiest way to get in touch. When I retired the first thing I did was bin my answering machine, so if you phone and no answer just call later. Always in evenings.

With very best wishes, thanks, and no I didn't miss it because I had no idea that it had gone.

Zombie – self inflicted RTA

Daily Telegraph, 31/10/14.

Jeffrey Stiles of Muskegon, Michigan, was clearly feeling pleased with the zombie costume he'd pulled together to attend a Halloween party last Saturday night. Stepping outside for a cigarette, the 45-year-old thought he'd take the fright fest to the next level and lurched onto the street in an attempt to scare drivers into thinking the undead apocalypse was underway.

It turns out he was more successful than anticipated.

According to reports, Stiles walked into the traffic lane and was promptly hit by a car. "He decided to walk along the roadway to scare cars, as he was dressed like a zombie for the Halloween party", confirms Ottawa County Sgt Matt Wilfong. "Though we don't know if the driver of the car was acting out a scene from *The Walking Dead* or simply didn't see Stiles, it appears he or she was sufficiently spooked and quickly fled the scene."

Stiles survived the hit-and-run with minor injuries and is currently recovering in an area hospital. Authorities are asking for any witnesses to come forward.

Leonardo self-portrait

The Independent, 3/5/2014.

Scientists are close to deciding how to restore a fading chalk sketch believed to be the only existing self-portrait by Leonardo da Vinci, following a hi-tech study of the paper.

The portrait, thought to be more than 400 years old, remains locked in a vault in the Royal Library of Turin, Italy, where it is believed to be gradually vanishing as the red-chalk image blends against the ageing yellow paper. Now scientists from Italy and Poland are using sophisticated restoration techniques to measure how much light is reflected and absorbed by the image.

Joanna Lojewska, of Jagiellonian University in Kraków, Poland, said: "This phenomenon is known as 'yellowing', which causes severe damage and negatively affects the aesthetic enjoyment of ancient artworks on paper."

Inflammatory beheading story

The Sun, 18/11/14.

Palmira Silva was found dead outside a house in Edmonton yesterday after police received calls that a man was attacking an animal and car with a knife. The "sweet" 82-year-old widow was found "collapsed" at the scene.

The suspect, who remains under police guard in hospital, was Tasered and arrested on suspicion of murder at the scene in Nightingale Road by armed officers, some of whom were injured in a struggle.

Scotland Yard have not yet confirmed the motive, but have emphasised that the incident did not appear to be terror-related, following the beheading of two American journalists by Islamic State militants in recent weeks.

The Sun story quoted sources who described the man as a "Muslim convert" who had "recently grown a beard." The tabloid's article has been described as "fear-mongering" by some, with many accusing the paper of inciting hatred against Muslims. An insider who worked with the suspect told the paper that the 25-year-old man "converted to Islam around April time. One of his parents was Muslim and he talked about praying. He put on a robe and prayed even when he was at work."

Fag-end

Dr Richard Wood

To USB (not Indy): Words 795.

A reflective tale from 2014.

In 1967 I was studying medicine at St Mary's Hospital in Praed St, Paddington, the heartland of London's drug, prostitution, sleezy film industry and the paradise for Rupert Murdoch's hacks. Not so widely talked of, it was also the heartland of second-hand shops' Harrods. Junk Shops that today's Antiques Road Show would give their eye teeth for.

In 'casulty', now called A&E, heroin addicted whores were our staple night time diet, a few often would come in with minor injuries from some professional (their profession) altercation and I well remember three am one night a fifteen-year-old girl with a broken hypodermic needle stuck in her arm. Despite the X-ray I and a colleague couldn't retrieve it using local anaesthetic, finally resorting to GA. Even now nearly fifty years later I can't see how you break a needle without bending it back and forth several times. That was Paddington then. I imagine nowadays it'll be all poshed up, populated by television news presenters, Channel Four's documentary makers, even the BBC. Who knows? When I worked there, down-town all right but character; no one could argue that.

Mary's is famous for two things; where (Sir) Alexander Fleming is erroneously said to have discovered penicillin in 1928 (blue plaque outside the hospital entrance). Actually the Crusaders, centuries earlier, found that mouldy bread on their wounds helped them heal, but they've never got credit for that (it is obscurely documented but you won't find that on The Internet). Remember all penicillin is is mould (cleaned up a bit of course).

Secondly it is where the world's first successful kidney transplant was done, the kidney shipped at high speed in a polythene bag from a fatal road accident and our path lab swiftly got their finger out and found it to be compatible with the patient (pure luck). I don't think anyone had the time, thought or interest to bugger about with relatives' permission. Nowadays I s'pose the hospital would be sued immediately (courtesy USA). The long-term life saved

189

seemed what mattered, in fact that's all we were interested in.

At this point I must paint a picture of the population in general's as well as the medical profession's view of smoking: in short there was no view. Smoking was then a climate we don't even get light from. Within medical circles smoking was exactly as prevalent as in the population at large; that's to say, give or take, fifty/fifty. I know somebody here will try to correct me but I really don't care – it'll make no difference to my tale and the chances they weren't there anyway.

Furthermore, and this perhaps is a little surprising: the social context mattered not a jot. Our tiered lecture theatres had ash trays on the back of the seat in front just as in cinemas and theatres. We students and consultant lecturers smoked through lectures. He or she had a tin ashtray on the desk in front of them. In the corridors and, not amongst the patients themselves, but certainly in the ward office, doctors, nurses and war sister (the all-overseeing dragon to both doctors, senior and junior, as well as her own staff).

Now in those days our anatomy was learnt on complete dead bodies, preserved in huge refrigerated tanks of formaldehyde. The bodies lay on long rows of heavy duty Formica-covered benches like a large McDonalds, between which the overseeing surgeon would wander constantly up and down answering questions and just chatting. There were four of us to a table (i.e. a body). Everything was very informal, jokes and humour presided. And just as in lectures smokers smoked throughout. Here there were no ashtrays so fags were simply stubbed out on the floor or in the flesh itself, the end thrown on the floor.

So I just end with the vivid memory of our consultant surgeon of the day, quite high profile on the National stage, as by definition they all were in a teaching hospital, walking past with a nonchalant smile, turning to stub his fag out leaving the end steaming from the a recently vacated eye socket.

Excuse the cliché but they were good days. I read only a couple of weeks ago that there is a current shortage of young doctors taking the root of surgery because they simply can't learn anatomy from computer models and pictures. Of course they can't. Texture and feel are paramount – that's pretty obvious. Any surgeon would tell them that from their sleep.

The two hospitals who've started this approach, Chester and one other, refused to give any comment to the press on the subject.

Carbon fibre and musical instruments

Carbon fibre has amongst other things, become a very fashionable material; the nineteen seventies and eighties.

It's extremely strong and extremely light. Perfect for example in the world of cycle racing – the one huge exception here is involvement in an accident. Crashes within the race itself are an everyday event and rarely cause much injury because everybody's going in the same direction. But with an on-coming motor vehicle, a very different story. Here a fracture (the bike not rider) and resulting injury with extremely sharp, jagged frame parts, infection? – high risk.

But to a completely different world: that of musical instruments where carbon fibre has become of huge interest especially in America. Here a luthier has one viewpoint: wood has no memory whatsoever. Carbon fibre does have a memory (in context-relative terms) comparable to that of a computer. That is to say that from his or her standpoint wood bends, carbon fibre doesn't. When you bend a wooden lute rib using heat it stays bent showing no inclination to return to its original straightness.

Not so carbon fibre – it would try to return to its previous state. I must quickly qualify this by making it clear that my own position is one of an amateur or small time luthier, and this text is so based. From this it is reasonable to say that carbon fibre is a material largely confined to industrial and professional applications. Turbine blades, piping, boat building and a large number of applications where its corrosion, albeit complete weather resistance and rigidity are a prerequisite. And all this requires moulding, temperature control facilities and production paraphernalia usually well beyond the financial reach of the small instrument-building endeavour.

The material itself is comprised of carbon crystals aligned in a longitudinal axis and is available in a huge variety of forms, from many textured or woven sheets, piping, to plain sheet, usually with some form of textured surface. Its rigidity (resistance to bending) is exceptionally high, but when it does fail – it fails catastrophically, as in the beginning of this text.

Now to lutherie. Wood has one intrinsic flaw – it moves and there's nothing you can do about that – there never has been and there never will be. Why? Because wood is ambient-humidity-dependent. Wooden furniture, musical instruments, anything you like made from wood; ambient humidity holds the trump card, which sometimes you can cleverly hold at bay (before you jump to varnish/oil/French polish – the insides of draws, instruments are uncoated).

The most common example here is with violins, guitars and stringed wooden instruments – the soundboard is constructed in two halves – 'book-matched' with the narrower tighter grain towards the centre line, wider grain towards the outside; this minimises humidity-related differential changes in the soundboard's dimensions.

Now carbon fibre completely wipes that scenario off the screen.

Research so far in the violin family carbon fibre has produced a different sound to conventional wooden examples; hardly surprising. Such words as stronger and louder have been bandied about but musicologists will no doubt lend precision to that. The other side of the equation being Strads and Amatis. The interesting thing is of course that it's not an equation – it's a completely new dimension. That's the whole point. Loudness relates to the amplitude of the oscillations of the belly at any given frequency.

Carbon fibre's characteristics allow for a thinner belly – in a guitar say even one millimetre. And what about the braces? are they needed at all? All for much more experimentation. The highly complex curvatures of the violin distinctly point toward commercial production, guitars also though admittedly they're far simpler.

The thing that most are agreed upon is that should you happen to be a member of the London Philharmonic Orchestra, booked for one night at The Royal Albert Hall in London, a few days later in a concert hall in the town of Manaus (bang in the middle of the Amazon rain forest), you probably wouldn't have to do that much re-tuning if you were using a carbon fibre instrument.

But – yes but. There's always a 'but'. The building 'vacancy' left for us single luthiers is simply the soundboard itself. So far I've discussed the building of complete instruments – yet a hybrid of wooden body and carbon fibre soundboard offers great things in the realm of aesthetics before even thinking of the acoustics.

I have a balalaika which has been sitting in the wings of my workbench for a about three years, its components mostly cut (from cherry) and now I've just decided – soundboard from carbon fibre with holly purfling (very light yellow to white). For me? an entirely new experience.

RHW, 2015.

Community radio appearance

To Chris Egerton, Lute Society,
ref. interview on Resonance104.4fm *community radio show based in east London.*

cc Steph.

16.10.14

Dear Chris,

Many thanks for your email – sorry to miss you on the 4th, but all your points taken on board. Don't worry, I'm perfectly well versed to behaving in/on public, swearing etc…(I do – normally with people I know – but…)

And doctors? Let me assure you if you think doctors go out when they've finished work and talk about how "... how that operation went this morning..." Oh no, no. They just go to the pub and get pissed like everybody else. It's only on telly that they're all serious. I've heard far quicker, wittier and crude jokes while taking out a gall bladder cancer than in the pub the same evening, and of course they're spontaneous.

There is however one problem that you and Steph will have to help me with. I know nothing about Renaissance music and certainly have no CDs of it. Classical music yes, but not Renaissance, and classical you said NOT. As I think you must have picked up – I'm not musical at all, in the sense that I don't play anything, neither do I have any wish to. My interest lies entirely with building which as I argue in one of those texts, has no logical connection with playing whatsoever.

Having said that, that in itself might be worth mentioning; we'll see at the coffee chat. From what you've said a couple of times she's pretty good at putting the show together with what's available, or rather adjusting what's available to what's needed... Surely Steph or you could provide the CDs as you think appropriate and we can talk about the music.

I have two lutenist friends who have played me what must be Renaissance music, and I've had plenty to say, and it's discussion that usually makes things interesting and discussion comes from all directions – by definition. You'll see I've copied her in with this email. I'm sure we'll be in contact before November, especially on the subject of playing music. Steph please note when you get this copy. Talk nearer the time.

Best to you both,
Richard.

Mars mission *one-way*

The Independent, 4/6/14.

Tuesday 10th September 2013.

Over 200,000 people from more than 140 countries have applied for a one-way ticket to Mars despite the seven-month journey in the hope of establishing the first human colony, but only four can become the first human settlers on the Red Planet. The astronauts are set to lift off in 2022.

The organisers of the *Mars One* mission announced that 202,586 people have submitted videos explaining why they should be chosen for the £4 billion project.

The plan to recoup the huge outlay is to create a media event that is more like an Olympics spectacular than a TV reality show.

"This mission to Mars can be the biggest media event in the world", said Paul Römer, the co-creator of *Big Brother* and ambassador of the project on the website. "Reality meets talent, show with no ending and the whole world watching. Now there's a good pitch."

The organisers say human settlement on Mars will aid our understanding of the origins of the solar system, the origins of life and our place in the universe. The *Mars One* website states the mission is only one-way as Earth return vehicles that can take off from the Red Planet are currently unavailable and would add to the already huge cost.

The privately-financed spaceflight project is led by Dutch entrepreneur Bas Lansdorp.

"We're not looking for individuals, we are looking for perfect teams. We want individuals who fit into certain teams of people going to Mars. They must be healthy, smart enough to learn new skills and with a character and mind-set that can function in a small group", Mr Lansdorp said.

Of the applicants who wanted the one-way ticket to Mars, the majority came from the United States, 47,654 from the US with 8,497 from Britain.

A selection committee will begin to sort the applicants and those chosen will have to pass three more rounds before the final decision.

The fourth, and final, round will be an international competition that prepares groups of candidates for life on Mars. At the end of the selection process, 24 individuals will be selected to become *Mars One* astronauts, and the four astronauts selected to become the first human settlers on Mars will land on the planet by 2023.

The plan is to build teams of four people, each from a different continent, who will live and train together for seven years before the first manned launch in 2022, arriving the following year.

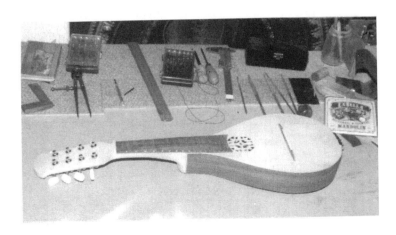